1977

Merry Christmas Johnny —
from Uncle George —
Aunt Julie

HOW DO THEY RUN IT?

WESTMINSTER PRESS BOOKS

BY

GEORGE SULLIVAN

How Do They Make It?
How Do They Grow It?
More *How Do They Make It?*
How Do They Run It?

HOW
DO THEY RUN IT?

by
GEORGE SULLIVAN

THE WESTMINSTER PRESS
Philadelphia

ISBN 0–664–32480–0

LIBRARY OF CONGRESS CATALOG CARD No. 73–121764

BOOK DESIGN BY
DOROTHY ALDEN SMITH

PUBLISHED BY THE WESTMINSTER PRESS®
PHILADELPHIA, PENNSYLVANIA

PRINTED IN THE UNITED STATES OF AMERICA

CONTENTS

INTRODUCTION

How is a "pogo stick" important to the operation of a supermarket? How does the owner of a drugstore set the price on a bottle of cologne? How do porcupines harass ski area managers?

How Do They Run It? answers these questions and countless others in telling about the operation of eleven different American business enterprises and public service institutions.

Management involves much more than simply directing or supervising. Management entails buying—knowing what to buy, how much to buy, and from whom—hiring, selling, advertising, record-keeping, and maintenance. How Do They Run It? focuses upon each one of these topics.

1

BOWLING CENTER

THE BOWLING BUSINESS went through a period of startling change not many years ago. This revolution had a sharp effect on the way every bowling center is operated and managed.

Bowling ranks as one of the most ancient of all sports. Relics of a game not unlike bowling have been found in the tombs of Egyptian rulers dating to the year 5200 B.C. Known by such names as skittles, lawn bowling, Dutch pins, bowls, ninepins, and tenpins, the game has been common to almost every culture through the centuries.

Bowling came to this country with the Dutch settlers of the seventeenth century. They called their version of the game ninepins. The Bowling Green section of lower Manhattan owes its name to the sport.

Through the centuries that followed the arrival of the Dutch, bowling alternately rose and fell in popularity. During the 1840's, gambling on the game became so prevalent that several states outlawed bowling. According to legend, bowlers of the day merely added

From the earliest times right up until the mid-1950's, the pinboy (left) was an integral part of the world bowling scene
NEW YORK PUBLIC LIBRARY

a tenth pin to the setup to get around the letter of the law. The new game —tenpins—is the one we play today.

The bowling business went through its period of radical change about twenty years ago. The automatic pinspotter is what triggered the revolution. Before the early 1950's, bowling

*The automatic pinspotter triggered a revo-
lution in the bowling business*

pins were always reset by hand. It was backbreaking work and the pay was small. Then in 1951, after decades of research, the automatic pinspotter was introduced. An electromechanical device, it set the pins and returned the ball, and it did both more quickly and more efficiently than a human could.

Best of all, the automatic machine was always available, summer or winter, day or night. The human pinboy was a disappointment in this regard. Sometimes he was late for work and other times he did not show up at all. But with the automatic pinspotter, the bowling center operator only had to flick a switch and the lane was ready for the customer to bowl.

The automatic pinspotter meant that the bowling center could operate at full capacity day or night, seven days a week. "The machine put the bowling proprietor on a par with other retailers in the community," says an industry official. "He now had a product to sell, like cornflakes. His shelves were always fully stacked. Success in the business meant moving merchandise, that is, in getting people to bowl."

To get people to bowl—that is the chief goal of the bowling center manager today. He has many duties, but his job of salesman is foremost.

When a new bowling center opens, the manager's first task is to organize his evening bowling leagues. A league is simply a group of teams, as few as four, or as many as the bowling center has room for, that bowls each week at a specified time in accordance with rules set down by the American Bowling Congress.

The bowling center enters into a formal contract with each league, promising to have a certain number of lanes available each week at a certain time, along with pins and other necessary equipment. The league pledges to pay the center an agreed-upon amount each week, and to bowl at the appointed time.

If the bowling center is located near an industrial plant, the proprietor will visit the plant and suggest to the recreation director that a group of plant employees form a league. Various departments of the plant will be invited to form teams. Usually there are five bowlers to a team.

The   manager   forms   additional

10

leagues by contacting other businesses in the area. He also calls upon fraternal groups, such as the local Rotary Club or Kiwanis Club. He will contact churches and sports clubs. The next time you visit your local bowling center, look at the league standings board that is posted there. Read the names of the leagues and teams. You will see they represent a cross section of the commercial and social activity of your community.

It is usually not difficult for the proprietor to fill his bowling center with leagues between the hours of six o'clock to eleven o'clock in the evening, Monday through Friday. Most people find it convenient to bowl between these hours.

But "moving merchandise," that is, getting people to bowl at other periods of the day, or other days of the week, is not quite so simple. Yet the manager must attract a good amount of off-hour business, as it is termed, in order to enjoy a profit.

If the bowling center is located in a suburban area, the manager will attempt to organize housewives' leagues on weekday mornings or early in the afternoon. Some bowling centers seek to encourage this type of business by serving women bowlers free coffee and providing free baby-sitting services. A nursery in a bowling center is no rarity. The proprietor will also have an instructor on hand to assist women who may never have bowled, or to lend a helping hand to those who know the fundamentals of the game but wish to improve their score.

What other types of off-hour leagues does the manager organize? It depends upon the type of community in which the bowling center is located. If it is located near a plant where the employees work on around-the-clock shifts, then the manager may be able to schedule a league at midnight, that is, right after the late shift finishes work. In metropolitan areas, some bowling centers draw off-hour leagues from groups of taxicab drivers or waiters.

While leagues provide the nucleus of a bowling center's business, a good amount of business is also derived from "open bowling." Open bowlers are nonleague bowlers. Usually they consist of groups of friends or families who visit the center on weekend afternoons or evenings to bowl a few games.

Bowling center managers work diligently with teen-age groups

Some bowling centers seek to encourage open bowling by advertising in local newspapers or on local radio stations.

Much of the manager's promotion effort is directed toward the development of junior bowlers. Boys and girls between the ages of eight and eighteen are encouraged to bowl in junior leagues, conducted after school or on weekends.

Many teen-agers like to bowl on dates. Most bowling centers invite parents to celebrate Junior's birthday with a "Happy Go Bowling" party. Party guests enjoy hamburgers, French fries, a soft drink, a slice of birthday cake and, of course, a game or two of bowling.

Almost every center has its own method of promoting junior bowling. An East Meadow, New York, proprietor offers a "Father and Son" bowling league. The league was introduced in 1964, and it now is the largest of its type in the country, with ninety-six fathers and ninety-six sons competing every Sunday morning, and a long list of people waiting to join.

In every type of promotion, proprietors work closely with one or more of the various organizations that make up the bowling industry. In the promotion of junior bowling, for instance, the proprietor enlists the cooperation of the American Junior Bowling Congress.

The AJBC supervises the operation of junior bowling leagues and tournaments, and it also operates a nation-wide instruction program for youngsters. Almost one thousand communities throughout the United States now have AJBC representation, and close to half a million youngsters hold membership in the organization.

Sometimes the owner of a bowling center or a group of owners will encourage local school administrators to teach students to learn to bowl as part of their gym program. "We've found that physical education specialists think very highly of bowling," says a Boston, Massachusetts, proprietor. "They realize the sport has an important 'carry-over' value. You can learn it as a youngster and play it throughout your adult life. This isn't true with most other American sports. A person seldom competes in baseball or football once he leaves college."

All this promotion activity has had a strong effect upon the quality of junior bowling. With more boys and girls bowling in organized competition than ever before, it is only natural that some outstanding scoring achievements have been recorded. During the 1968–1969 season, thirteen-year-old Dave Razzari, of San Mateo, California, became the youngest bowler ever to roll a 300 game in league competition. Another young San Mateo bowler, sixteen-year-old Rick Celotti, became the first junior bowler to roll 300's in consecutive league sessions.

That's not all. During the 1968–1969 season, the highest score bowled in league competition among all bowlers, juniors *and* adults, was turned in

Many youngsters learn the fundamentals of bowling in school gym class

by seventeen-year-old Wayne Chester. Bowling in a Daly City, California, league, Wayne rolled an astounding 847 for three games, only 53 pins short of perfection.

The way in which a bowling center is operated varies somewhat with its size. A small center, one that has eight to sixteen lanes, may be owned by one individual, and managed by that person too. But a larger bowling center, ranging up to thirty-two or forty-eight lanes in size, is almost certain to be owned by several individuals. They employ a manager to supervise day-to-day operations.

It is up to the manager to have competent employees and to see that they are properly trained. He supervises each person and evaluates performances regularly, recommending increases for those qualified.

The manager sets the hours the bowling center will operate, and establishes working hours for each of the employees. Some personnel work on a full-time basis, but others, like a deskman or an assistant mechanic, may be only part-time employees.

The manager also sets certain rules and regulations the employees must follow. Are employees allowed use of the office telephone? Are employees allowed to smoke or drink during working hours? Are they to receive discount rates when they bowl or buy merchandise? Are they to receive overtime pay or bonuses at Christmas? It is up to the manager to set the policy in such matters.

All expenditures have to be approved by the manager, everything from maintenance supplies to replacement parts for the automatic pinspotters.

The manager's staff numbers from five to fifteen employees, depending upon the size of the bowling center. He has a mechanic to maintain and repair the automatic pinspotters, a lane maintenance man to keep the alleys in playable condition, and a building maintenance man to keep the establishment clean. He also employs a bowling instructor and a counter control man, often called a deskman.

Many managers believe that the counter control man is the most important of all their employees. He is the bowling center's goodwill ambassador, the man whose job it is to make each customer feel welcome.

"Good evening, sir. May I help you?" he says to each one. He is well-groomed. He is cheerful and smiles easily. He shows a genuine interest in the needs of each customer.

The deskman's most important duty is to assign customers to lanes and to collect their money when they have finished bowling. This is the most carefully controlled of all operations within the bowling center.

As one facet of the control system, the deskman keeps watch over a battery of small meters, one for each pinspotter. Each meter registers the number of frames bowled. (A frame is like an inning in baseball; there are ten frames of bowling to each game.)

When the customer is assigned a lane, the deskman reads the meter for the customer's lane, and enters the reading in the space provided in one corner of the score sheet. When the customer finishes bowling and brings his score sheet to the desk, the counter-man reads the meter again. The difference between the two readings represents the frames bowled, and the deskman charges the customer accordingly.

In addition to the meters at the desk, there is a meter on each pinspotter. It also keeps track of the frames bowled. But this meter is sealed; it cannot be set back or advanced except by a factory mechanic. The manager of the bowling center uses this meter as an additional check that he

is receiving payment for each frame bowled.

On an active day, a bowling center of only average size can attract many hundreds of people. The manager realizes that being busy causes his cash register to play a happy tune, but that heavy traffic also brings on headaches, many more headaches than a similar number of people might cause for the manager of a supermarket or a motion picture theater.

People who visit a bowling center have a wide assortment of very special needs. Each group requires a pair of lanes on which to bowl and automatic pinspotting machines that are in top-flight working condition. This is just the beginning.

A person can't wear street shoes when he bowls, so the deskman must give out—rent—special bowling shoes. (The left shoe has a leather sole, allowing the bowler that vital slide on the last step of his delivery, while the sole of the right shoe is rough-surfaced and serves to brake the bowler's approach.) Each bowler in the group must find a bowling ball that fits properly. The party requires a score sheet and a scoring pencil.

Once the group is properly outfitted and begins bowling, they are likely to order food and drink. This means, unless employees are watchful, an unsightly clutter of cups, glasses, and dishes.

Bowlers are active people, and this activity creates dust. Tile areas have to be swept down often when the bowling center is busy. Carpeted areas have to be vacuumed. Ashtrays have to be emptied constantly.

"Cleanliness is just as vital to the success of a bowling center as heating and air conditioning," says a bowling management expert. When the bowling center closes at night, it gets a thorough cleaning from top to bottom. Hard-surfaced floors are swept and mopped. Carpeting is vacuumed and spot-cleaned wherever necessary. Ashtrays are washed. Bowling balls are returned to their storage racks. Settees, tables, and chairs are dusted and polished. Parking lot debris is collected. Scoring pencils are sharpened. "After you've been in this business for a while, you begin to feel like a janitor," says a Midwest proprietor. "But you have no choice. You have to keep the place clean. Otherwise, you might as well close up."

At the same time the bowling area is being rendered spotless, the machine maintenance man is working on the automatic pinspotters—adjusting some parts, and cleaning and lubricating others. He follows a precise schedule of both daily and weekly maintenance chores.

The lanes themselves must be cleaned and prepared for next day's bowling—a procedure called "dressing." This job is done by the lane maintenance man.

When a lane is dressed, it gets a thin coating of oil. This keeps the lane wood from drying out. It also helps the bowler to achieve good scores. If the lane had little or no oil, there would be too much friction between the ball and the lane, and the ball would be difficult to control. Too much oil is just as bad. Then the ball slides, and again the bowler has difficulty controlling it. So the lane maintenance man has to be careful that he puts down just the right amount of oil. It is not a job that can be done by an inexperienced person.

The lane maintenance man begins by cleaning the lane, wiping it down with a special long-handled duster. Using a spray gun, he then applies the

A business bowling center requires efficient management and unrelenting maintenance

dressing. Starting from a point not far from the pins, he walks backward toward the foul line, holding the spray gun about eighteen inches above the lane while it hisses out a fine fog of oil. Less than one quarter of an ounce of oil is used on each lane.

Then the maintenance man polishes the lane, using a big rotary buffer. He makes two trips up and down the length of each lane.

You can check the amount of oil on a lane by running a finger over its surface. If the lane has the proper amount of oil, a faint smudge will appear. If there is no smudge, the lane is too dry. If the lane feels oily, it has an excess of dressing or has not been properly buffed.

Bowling pins also require a great deal of care. "The average bowler has no idea how much pins cost, nor of the amount of time and effort spent maintaining them," says Jack Moran, manager of Morris-Essex Lanes in Florham Park, New Jersey.

A bowling pin is constructed of laminated chunks of hard rock maple. These are sanded into pin shape and then sheathed in thin rugged plastic.

The American Bowling Congress sets pin specifications. The approved pin is 15 inches tall. Its diameter is 2 ¼ inches at the base and 4 ¾ inches at the widest point. A wood pin with plastic skin must weigh between 3 pounds, 2 ounces, and 3 pounds, 10 ounces, but within each set of ten, the individual pins cannot vary more than four ounces.

Ten bowling pins—a "set"—cost about $50. Each automatic pinspotter requires two sets. Thus, to equip a 32-lane bowling center with pins enough to allow bowling on every lane requires an expenditure of $3,200. But often the figure climbs to twice this amount. In order to care for the pins properly, they must be rested periodically. "Pins are something like humans," says Jack Moran. "Every now and then they have to be taken out of service and allowed to catch their breath. Otherwise, they don't last very long."

This means, of course, that each lane requires four sets of pins, not two. Two sets are in use while the other two are resting. So the cash outlay to equip a 32-lane center with pins is $6,400.

Resting the pins periodically is only one part of the proprietor's pin maintenance program. He also sees to it that the pins are washed regularly in special solvents so they will always appear shining-white to the bowler. The proprietor also has the pins coated with special lacquers so that they will be resilient and produce high scores. When a pin's plastic jacket develops a worn spot or cracks, it must be patched. Broken bottoms must be replaced with new ones.

Great care has to be exercised in storing pins. They must be kept where it is cool and dry. Pins stored in conditions of high humidity soak up moisture and are much less resilient when put into use. Bowlers find "heavy" pins difficult to topple. Scores plummet and loud complaints result.

Nearly every bowling center offers some type of food-serving facility. It may be simply a snack bar where soft drinks and sandwiches are sold, or it might be a small coffee shop offering light meals. A few large bowling centers boast elegant restaurants.

While bowling center owners recognize that they must be equipped to serve their customers food and beverages, many of them do not wish to assume the duties and responsibilities that go with a restaurant operation, no matter how modest the operation might be. For this reason most owners lease the food service operation to a person with experience in the field. The concessionaire pays the owner of the bowling center a percentage of the snack bar's gross sales in return for the floor space and use of the equipment. A common figure is 15 percent of the sales.

Yet even though he leases out the operation, the owner has to be careful to maintain a certain amount of control. If the concessionaire does not measure up in terms of food quality or efficient service, it reflects upon the bowling center as a whole. "You have to be the boss," says a Paramus, New Jersey, bowling proprietor. "If someone comes in and gets served an overcooked hamburger or greasy French fries, I'm the one who gets blamed, not the concessionaire.

"You have to exercise great care in selecting someone to run your snack bar. It's almost like choosing a business partner."

In many areas of the United States, the bowling business is extremely competitive. Not only do bowling centers within a given trading area compete with one another, but they also vie with other entertainment enterprises for the customer's dollar. The local motion picture theater, golf courses, and skating rinks offer competition.

Millions of people would rather watch television than bowl. "We can tell when there's an important Green Bay Packers football game being telecast on a Sunday afternoon," says the operator of a Milwaukee bowling center, "because our lanes will be almost empty. But as soon as the game is over, the people flock in."

According to the American Bowling Congress, there were 9,378 bowling centers in operation in the United States in 1969. There were 10,883 centers in operation in 1963. In other words, 1,505 bowling centers went out of business between 1963 and 1969.

What happened? Some fell victim to the severe competition. A few were destroyed by fire or some other natural disaster. But many failed because of poor management. "Sound management—that's the key to success in this business," says an industry official. "It's as necessary as pins, balls, and maple lanes."

2

COMMUNITY PHARMACY

THE DICTIONARY defines pharmacy as the science of preparing and dispensing drugs. It is an art that dates to the earliest of times.

Primitive man valued certain plants for their healing and curative powers, and the knowledge of these remedies was passed from generation to generation. Today, most of our drugs are prepared synthetically, but many drug plants continue to be of value. From cinchona bark we obtain quinine, used in the treatment of malaria. From the dried leaves of the foxglove plant we derive digitalis, a drug used as a heart stimulant. Castor oil comes from the castor bean, and camphor from the camphor tree.

The science of pharmacy was practiced in ancient Egypt, Greece, and Rome. Sorcery and superstition shrouded the trade in those long past

This Egyptian drawing of an ancient ointment seller is from the tomb of Kagemi, and dates to around 2400 B.C.

times. Egyptian drug mixers used drawings of the Eye of Horus, a sungod, to ward off sickness and disease.

The sign continued to be used during the Middle Ages, although it was modified in such a way that it resembled the figure 4. Physicians of the time inscribed their formulas with the mark, hoping it would assure them the protection of Jupiter, the god of the heavens and of weather.

Through the centuries, the mark was further modified until it looked like this: R_x. Today, the symbol is often found on prescription blanks, or it may shine in bright neon as the symbol of a community pharmacy itself.

The science of preparing drug remedies was well known in this country before the landing of the first English colonists. The American Indians used 144 different drugs in the treatment of sickness and diseases, and 59 of these are still regarded as effective medicinal preparations.

From the earliest days, the practice of pharmacy and that of medicine were closely allied. This was true in colonial America, where early pharmacists were also physicians. A man who practiced this dual profession was known by the English term "apothecary." To William Davis goes the credit for opening the first apothecary shop in the United States. It was established in Boston in 1646.

Pharmacy and medicine were not established as separate professions in the United States until the nineteenth century. The first college of pharmacy is of fairly recent origin, starting in 1821 in the city of Philadelphia. Training in pharmacy was not generally available until many years after, and the term "pharmacist" itself did not come into general use until after 1870.

A boy or girl high school graduate who wishes to become a pharmacist begins by enrolling in a college of pharmacy, first making certain that the college is one approved by the American Council on Pharmaceutical Education. Usually the period of schooling is five years, with one year devoted to liberal arts schooling and four years to training in pharmacy. During this period the candidate studies such subjects as anatomy, chemistry, biology, physiology, and mathematics—all subjects that deal directly with the preparation, use, and effect of drugs.

Once the individual has earned his degree, he is recognized as a professional, as an expert in his chosen field. But under the law of most states, he is still not qualified to prepare and dispense drugs. He must serve an apprenticeship period, which varies from six months to a year. In some ways it is comparable to the period of internship a physician must serve.

During the period of apprenticeship, the pharmacist may prepare prescriptions, but only under the supervision of a pharmacist already registered. He uses this period to gain experience, not only in the compounding of prescriptions but in every aspect of the management and operation of a retail pharmacy.

After serving his period of apprenticeship, the candidate must pass a series of written and oral examinations in the state in which he wishes to practice. Once he passes the examinations and pays the necessary licensing fees, he becomes "registered."

Then he is likely to spend several years working for other pharmacists before going into business for himself. If he is wise, he accumulates different kinds of experience. He may first work in a store that emphasizes the prescription side of the business, and then in another that stresses merchandising, promotion, and a high volume of sales. Later he might find it to his advantage to work for a drug wholesaler. In this way he becomes familiar with the thousands of drugs and drugstore items on the market. There is no substitute for experience, and it is the only way the young man can gain the knowledge necessary to operate a pharmacy of his own.

Like a physician or an attorney, the pharmacist is a professional person, one who has achieved his occupational goal through extensive education. But once he takes on the ownership of a pharmacy, he becomes a businessman, too, and he must learn to cope with the many and varied problems involved in the day-to-day management of his store. Nevertheless, his store's prescription department is the heart of his business.

The average community pharmacy compounds about fifty prescriptions a day, and prescription sales account for approximately 40 percent of the store's total sales volume. No other department is so important.

The prescription department is where the pharmacist spends most of his time, and the work area has to be planned with the utmost care. It has to provide great convenience, but at the same time it must assure a certain degree of privacy. "It can't be an area open to the public," as one pharmacist points out, "because cleanliness is so vital. In addition, we have to be able to concentrate when we compound a prescription, to work without being distracted."

In most cases, the store owner will locate his prescription-compounding area at the extreme rear of the store, separating it from the shopping area with a partition at least shoulder level in height. The work area itself is laid out so that the pharmacist faces the shopping area as he works. He may have to turn his back to take a drug from a supply drawer, but all the other tasks involved in compounding prescriptions—counting, sorting, mixing, and typing labels—can be performed while facing forward.

The reason for this is easy to see. The pharmacist wants to know when a customer enters the store. He wants to be able to recognize when a customer needs sales help. By facing forward he is also better able to detect a shoplifter. Sometimes the pharmacist will raise the floor in the prescription department to give the area more of an observation-post character.

In some pharmacies the prescription department is completely hidden from the customer's view. But this type of arrangement is usually common only to large stores employing several pharmacists. It is rare in the store where the pharmacist is the owner-manager.

The working area within the prescription department is a model of efficiency. There is a broad, smooth-surfaced counter upon which the prescriptions are compounded. Labels hang in a roll above the typewriter. Prescription file cards are racked close by. The telephone is near at hand, but not on the counter. Lighting is bright and uniform.

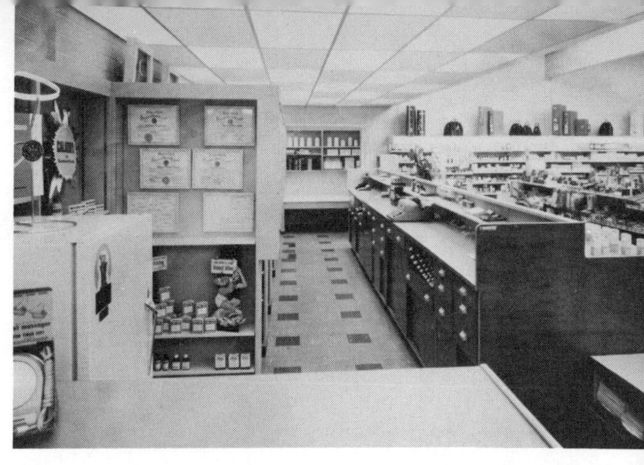

The prescription department has to be arranged carefully. Here the pharmacist's file drawers, storage drawers, sink, bottle rack, and other items of equipment are arranged for fast, efficient operation
MCKESSON & ROBBINS, INC.

The pharmacist keeps a careful record of all the prescriptions he fills. Most pharmacists give each one a serial number. It appears on the prescription label, on the customer's file card, and on the prescription slip from the doctor, which the pharmacist also keeps on file. So it is an easy matter for the pharmacist to refill a prescription, even if the patient loses the original label or it becomes defaced.

Special care has to be taken in the handling of narcotics. The Bureau of Narcotics and Dangerous Drugs exercises strict controls over the sale and distribution of morphine, cocaine, demerol, opium, and all other narcotic drugs. When purchasing narcotic supplies, the pharmacist must use official government order forms, and he is allowed to deal only with wholesalers and manufacturers who are licensed to sell narcotics.

The pharmacist's supply of narcotics must be stored in a safe place and

The pharmacist must keep a careful record of filled prescriptions

kept under tight inventory control. He is permitted to dispense narcotic drugs only when presented a prescription written by a qualified and registered medical practitioner. The pharmacist knows that federal inspectors will examine his narcotics records periodically.

The business of purchasing is critical in the operation of the community pharmacy. The pharmacy manager has to know what items his customers want, where to buy them and in what quantities, and how much to pay.

All retail pharmacists buy their supplies from drug wholesalers. If his store is in a large city, the manager has scores of wholesalers to choose from, but he will usually give most of his business to just two or three of the larger houses. If he tries to give some business to everybody, he finds himself involved in separate salesmen's calls, separate orders, separate deliveries, and separate bills. He becomes a full-time purchasing agent.

In addition to the drug wholesalers, the pharmacy manager is also likely to deal with a news distributor for newspapers, books, and magazines, and with a tobacco wholesaler for cigarettes, cigars, and candy. Sometimes a nationally known cosmetic firm will select a store to serve as an exclusive sales outlet in a trading area. This means that the store deals directly with the manufacturer in making its cosmetic purchases.

Purchasing stock for the prescription department presents special problems. The store owner would require a storeroom area the size of a supermarket parking lot if he tried to stock each one of the thousands upon thousands of drug items now offered. Yet he must keep a wide variety of stock on hand, for he realizes that every unfilled prescription means the loss of a sale plus, potentially, future business. Ordering the correct items and in the right amounts takes experience and keen judgment.

The store manager's problem is eased somewhat by the fact doctors in a given neighborhood prescribe the same drugs over and over again. Of course, new drugs are being introduced all the time, and doctors read about them and prescribe them.

Pharmacists do their buying from salesmen representing drug wholesalers

Every pharmacist maintains a "want book." During each business day he uses it to jot down items on which he is running low. It becomes his shopping list.

The "want book," however, is not enough in itself. The pharmacy manager also must keep alert to changing demands. Sometimes these are triggered by a change in season. For example, during July the store manager is likely to order large amounts of notebooks, stationery, pens, and pencils for delivery in August, a month in which he knows youngsters and their parents will be purchasing back-to-school supplies. No experienced store manager would go without ordering cold remedies for the winter months or suntan lotion for the summer.

The changing seasons are only one influence upon customer purchases. Sometimes a new product, heavily supported by national advertising, will nudge an established one aside in terms of customer preference. This happened in the toothpaste field in recent years. The drugstore manager has to keep alert to such changes in customer preferences.

"How *much* should I buy?" This is always a crucial question. If the store owner is too careful in making his purchases and limits quantities, he may quickly run out of needed items and so lose sales. But ordering too much is just as foolhardy. The wholesaler has to be paid for whatever is purchased. Should the store manager overorder, he ties up his capital needlessly and thus limits his profits.

All of this has to do with the subject of "turnover." Turnover is the rate at which the store's inventory, that is, all the items the store has stocked, is sold and restocked. The higher the rate of turnover, the less money the store manager has to invest in his inventory. So every store owner strives for a high turnover rate.

When a store boasts a high turnover, the manager needs less storage space and, in the store itself, less shelf space. More items can be handled as a result. There is also less likelihood that stock will become shopworn or damaged and have to be thrown out.

Aside from buying too much, many, many other factors contribute to a low turnover rate. Lack of proper stock records is one reason, along with the failure to take frequent inventories.

A low turnover rate can also result from prices that are too high, so high that there is buyer resistance. Pricing is another subject to which the store owner must give careful attention.

In setting prices, a "markup" is established for each item. Markup is defined as the amount the store manager adds to the cost of an item to cover his expenses and also provide him with a profit.

Markup is usually expressed as a percentage of the selling price. If the store owner knows that his expenses are 26 percent of his income, and he expects a 4 percent profit on sales, then he marks up his items by adding 30 percent to the wholesale cost.

As an example, take a bottle of cologne for which the store owner pays $2.00. If he wants to mark up the item 30 percent, he uses this formula:

$$\frac{\$2.00}{1.00 - .30} = \frac{\$2.00}{.70} = \$2.85$$

The price he charges for the cologne is $2.85. It would seem that the store manager could take each item in the store and apply this formula. He would then be guaranteed a return that would pay for the cost of the item, reimburse him for his expenses, and assure him of a profit. In practice, however, it is not quite this simple.

Price must also be related to several other factors. Some items take up only a tiny amount of shelf space; others are so large as to present storage problems. Storage space is a very real cost, and the king-size merchandise must be marked up higher.

Some goods, by their nature, turn over quickly, while others move sluggishly. Depreciation, the fact that some items decrease in value through ordinary wear and tear, is still another element that influences price.

In establishing a price schedule for his merchandise, the store manager works department by department. Let's take the cosmetic department as an example. On lipsticks, which represent an extremely high volume of sales and have a rapid turnover rate, the markup is small, perhaps only 7 or 8 percent. On perfume, which does not turn over so quickly, the markup is a bit higher, around 30 percent. Electric tooth-brushes and hair dryers, which also might be sold at the cosmetic counter, are slow-moving items and have a low turnover rate. On these the markup is higher still, perhaps as much as 20 or 30 percent.

Sometimes a store manager is forced into selling merchandise at a loss. He may make a misjudgment in ordering an item. His customers shun it, and it stays on the shelf month after month. He cannot afford to store the item endlessly, so he begins reducing the price, little by little. Finally it sells. But the return he receives may be less than the actual cost.

In recent years, as the country's economy has taken an inflationary trend, people in general have become more and more sophisticated about prices. They shop; they compare prices. They know which stores offer the best bargains.

Yet while low prices are a tried and proven method of attracting customers, every pharmacist knows that the matter of price is only one factor in holding a customer. People, he realizes, are willing to pay a few cents more for most items if the store offers more than the average in the way of service, personal attention, and a professional atmosphere. Even the most astute bargain hunters appreciate these qualities.

Occasionally a customer will want to quibble over a particular price. "It's just too much," he says. "I can get it at Johnson's Drugstore for a lot less."

The store owner realizes that this type of customer is probably giving the same story to every pharmacy in the neighborhood. A sharp-minded owner knows what his competitors are charging and never allows himself to be undersold to any great degree. When a customer suggests that he can do a great deal better elsewhere, the store manager will usually suggest that he take advantage of the amazing bargain.

Some people are born hagglers and want to bargain over everything they buy, right down to a package of chewing gum. But the manager has to discourage dickering. It may be acceptable when buying a used car or a piece of real estate, but in a community pharmacy the store manager sets the prices carefully and conscientiously—and then stands by them.

Shoplifting can be a serious problem for the community pharmacy. Because the store offers a large stock of small items that fit easily into the pocket or purse, it is always an inviting target for the dishonest person who sees something that he can't afford—or resist.

People suspected of shoplifting must be dealt with carefully. There is always a chance of injuring the feelings of a customer. When a salesperson notices somebody acting suspiciously, the usual procedure is for him to approach the individual and ask, "May I wrap that item for you?"

Or suppose a clerk feels that a person has browsed longer than seems necessary. "Are you having trouble? May I help you?" he can ask.

Stock control and periodic inventory are vital to drugstore operation

Two other topics are important in operating a community pharmacy. They are "stock control" and "inventory." Stock control refers to the day-to-day management and supervision of all merchandise items. Inventory is the periodic physical count of these items.

There are many types of stock control systems, but most stores maintain a file of stock cards, one card for each item sold. The card lists the item's purchase price, its selling price, the quantity in stock, and the quantity on order. The card may also carry information about the supplier, the usual quantity ordered, the price paid, and the terms. In the case of drug supplies, the items may be recorded in terms of number of capsules or tablets. Employees in each department are responsible for keeping their own stock cards up to date.

Taking inventory at regular intervals is as necessary to the pharmacy's efficient operation as a telephone and a cash register. By means of the inventory, the store manager is able to verify information on the stock control cards. It also is another method of controlling stock, for a careful inventory is sure to reveal several items that are almost out of stock and need to be reordered. The inventory also serves as another means of helping to detect shoplifting and pilferage.

Taking inventory is a time-consuming task, and most store managers perform the chore at night, after the store is closed. Employees work in pairs. One does the actual counting, calling out the total number for each item to the second clerk who keeps a tally sheet.

The store manager spot-checks the count, that is, he audits a random sampling of the figures reported by the clerks. This helps to keep the employees alert as to the importance of being accurate.

Maintaining stock control cards and taking careful periodic inventories are

Baby needs, cosmetics, deodorants, first-aid equipment, tobacco, candy—these are some of the items the modern pharmacy handles besides prescriptions

MCKESSON & ROBBINS, INC.

only one part of the record-keeping of the community pharmacist. He also has to keep accurate financial records. He usually hires a professional accountant or bookkeeper to handle this task.

Such records are essential in order for the store owner to know the condition of his business in terms of dollars and cents. How much of a profit is he actually earning? In what departments can the profit picture be improved? How much money is tied up in stock? What percentage of income is going for payroll, advertising, insurance, store maintenance, etc.? Carefully prepared financial records help to answer questions like these.

Records also help the store owner provide accurate information to the Internal Revenue Service, and state and local tax collectors. And they are still another method of checking or preventing shoplifting.

When it comes to competition, the owner of the pharmacy has more to worry about than just the other pharmacies within his trading area. Nowadays many other types of retail operations are engaged in the struggle for the customer who was once exclusively the drugstore's.

Most department stores now carry packaged medicine, toiletries, cosmetics, and greeting cards. These are all items that account for an important part of the sales volume in the average community pharmacy. Some department stores have established complete prescription departments.

You can now buy aspirin and some cough medicines in the supermarket. The local variety store stocks an imposing array of beauty products. Clothing stores offer men's grooming aids.

The community pharmacy has had to learn to cope with this growing trend. One way is to emphasize personal service. For instance, when it comes to the sale of beauty aids, an astute independent pharmacist will train his salespeople to answer women's questions on the application of cosmetics. Another way is by providing quick delivery.

A third way the community pharmacy meets competition from other types of retail outlets is by offering a wider range of merchandise. Many pharmacies now stock leather goods and luggage, toys, jewelry, stationery, glassware, and other products quite unrelated to the drug field.

Some people find fault with this policy. "A drugstore should sell just drugs," say the critics.

Of course, some pharmacies do compound and sell prescriptions and handle nothing else. These are known as professional pharmacies. They are usually located near clinics or hospitals, or in office buildings occupied largely by doctors or dentists.

In the great majority of cases, the independent pharmacist cannot depend on prescription business alone for his income. If he did not sell ice cream and toiletries, cosmetics and greeting cards, he would not be likely to survive for very long.

According to the Small Business Administration, there are approximately 55,000 retail pharmacies in the United States. But the number is not keeping pace with the country's ever-increasing population. Indeed, there is a growing shortage of registered pharmacists.

Some observers forecast that the days of the community pharmacies are numbered, that corner drugstores are going to be replaced by much bigger, ultramodern stores, each one serving a larger trading area. These stores will compound prescriptions, but this will be only a small part of their business, for each will offer a vast selection of merchandise items. Each will be like a small department store.

Other observers feel such stores have only limited appeal. "People appreciate the individual attention they receive in the smaller, neighborhood store," says Edward J. Zegarowicz, a New York City store owner. "In fact, they expect the store owner to deal with them on a personal, even confidential basis. A person doesn't get this kind of treatment in a big, multipurpose store. There'll always be a need for the community pharmacy."

3

SKI AREA

SKIING as we know it today is a relatively new sport. As recently as the mid-1930's, Vermont and New Hampshire had the country's only commercial ski areas, but today ski areas can be created almost anywhere in the United States,

In 1970, according to *Ski Area Management* magazine, there were a total of 780 ski areas in the United States and about 200 more in Canada, with the number increasing at the rate of about 3 or 4 percent each year.

Not every site with snow and skiers qualifies as a ski *area*. To be classified as a ski area, the enterprise must operate at least one tow or cable lift, the apparatus used for hauling skiers up a slope. The fact that ski areas operate lift equipment is one of the very few features they have in common. In character, ski areas cover a very wide range, and managing the ski area at Hickory Hill, New York, presents distinctly different problems from managing the one at Sun Valley, Idaho.

About one half the country's ski areas are located in the Northeast—in New England, New York, and Pennsylvania. Generally, the season begins in early December and lasts through March. The mountains of this section of the country, when compared to the awesomeness of the Rockies, are of rather modest size. New Hampshire's Mt. Washington, the highest in the state, reaches "only" 6,288 feet, while Colorado's Mt. Elbert, at 14,431 feet, is almost two and one half times as high.

Weather conditions are also different. The Eastern ski areas, excepting those in Maine, northern New York, Vermont, and New Hampshire, are victim to erratic conditions. It can be snowing and ideal for skiing one day, and raining and wretched the next.

Ski resorts of the Northeast draw heavily from the large cities of the area. Weekends are the busiest, with most people driving their own cars to areas.

There is also skiing to be found in the mid-Atlantic region of the country, with about a dozen resorts in North Carolina, Virginia, and Tennessee. But snow is something of a rarity in these states and the ski season is brief, only about ninety days in length.

The Midwest, particularly Michigan, Minnesota, and Wisconsin, can claim ample snow of high quality for skiing, and the season is extended from December into April. But the drawback in the Midwest is the terrain. A skier used to the magnificence of Rocky Mountain skiing might look upon the "mountains" of the Midwest as mere hills. The highest peak in Michigan is 2,023 feet; Indiana's is 1,240 feet.

As in the East, skiing in the Midwest is primarily a weekend activity. And because the slopes are usually gentle, many children ski.

The ski area business is very different in the Rocky Mountain West, in Colorado and Utah. There peaks soar high above the clouds and ski slopes are broad and long. The ski season is longer than in the East, stretching from mid-November into May.

Skiers rate Rocky Mountain snow as the best there is. It is light, dry, and powdery, and in some areas a fresh blanket falls every day.

A ski resort in the East might offer patrons a single lodge or two, a coffee shop, and a restaurant. But in Colorado and Utah, a ski area is likely to present an imposing complex of lodges and restaurants and a variety of other recreational activities. For example, near the city of Aspen, Colorado, there are more than seventy ski lodges and about half of them boast heated swimming pools and skating rinks.

People from every part of the United States enjoy Colorado skiing. The airlines bring in a steady flow of vacationers from New York City, Chicago, Detroit, and other population centers.

Skiing is also a major sport on the Pacific Coast. There are well over a hundred resorts sprinkled from Mount Baker near Bellingham, Washington, to the Big Bear Lake region of California, southeast of Los Angeles.

The most luxurious of California's resorts are clustered in the Lake Tahoe region of the High Sierra east of San Francisco. The peaks there are almost the equal of those in the Rocky Mountains, and the ski slopes and trails are to be found at altitudes between 5,000 and 9,000 feet.

Starting a new ski area, no matter where it is to be located, often requires an enormous amount of money, several million dollars in some cases. The bulk of it goes toward the purchase of land, the construction of buildings, and the installation of lift equipment. Ski areas are usually owned and operated by corporations. Members of the corporation, or the corporate directors, establish the basic operational guidelines for the area, then hire a manager to carry them out.

Operating a ski area may seem simple and not very expensive. You need cold weather, snow, and a long, steep incline—all of which nature provides. Next you need skiers, and, according to industry experts, skiers exist in abundance. Simply let the skiers know you are in business and the money will start rolling in.

Jammed parking lot at this California resort testifies to skiing's popularity

SQUAW VALLEY DEVELOPMENT CO.

The crawler is the basic piece of snow-grooming equipment

SQUAW VALLEY

This is a chair lift; the "bullwheel" is at left

UNITED AIR LINES

The gondola is the most elegant of lifts

SQUAW VALLEY

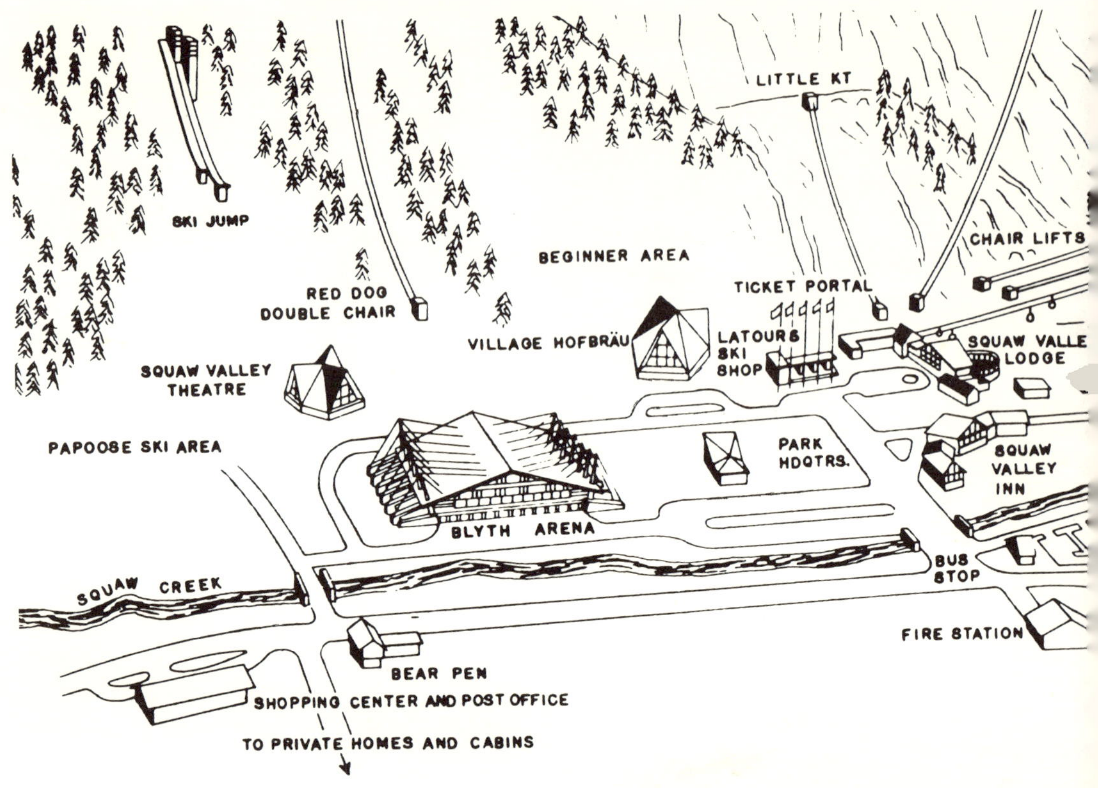

Squaw Valley, near Tahoe City, California, typifies the modern, many-faceted ski area

But it is not that easy. Snow, as basic to the sport as sloping land, can be a poignant problem. In the Northeast, Mother Nature does not always cooperate, and the ski area manager may be victimized by a snow drought lasting two or three weeks or even longer.

But ski area operators of the Northeast have solved this problem. They now make their own snow.

The art of snow-making was discovered by accident. One bitter cold December night in 1950, two Massachusetts farmers forgot to turn off a spray gun on their farm's irrigation equipment. The next morning the ground near the gun was covered with snow. The two men formed a company to manufacture and sell snow makers. It took many years for them to perfect the equipment and convince skeptics it was practical.

Owners of ski resorts began installing snow-making equipment during the mid-1960's. At first there was sharp resistance to the equipment. Installing the huge compressors necessary to pump the water to the slopes, the miles of metal pipes, and hoses and nozzles required a sizable outlay of cash, as

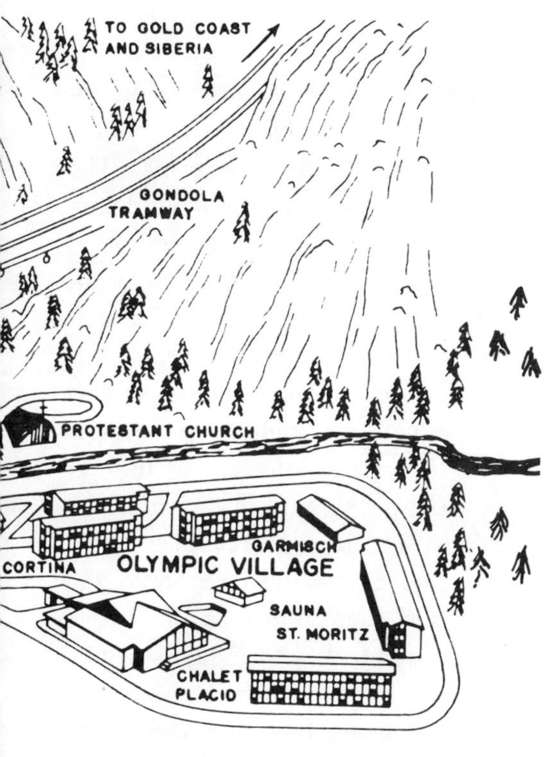

mont. "We felt the ski business had become so big that it would be foolhardy to take a chance on missing the big business we always do at Christmas and in the spring just because nature failed to come through."

In covering a slope with artificial snow, the first step is to set the equipment in position. Each snow "gun" is mounted on a tripod and linked by a hose and underground pipe to the pumphouse. Each one of several hill workers may be assigned as many as ten guns. On a long slope, the guns are first positioned near the top of the hill, then moved in stages toward the base.

When the guns are in position, air is sent through the lines. Then the hill worker calls for water. The mixture of water and air produces snow. But the mix has to be right. Too much water produces slush. Too much air, and a light, nonskiable powder spews forth.

The amount of water also has to be regulated with an eye toward the day's temperature and humidity. When the temperature and humidity drop, more water is needed, and when conditions are the reverse, less water.

As the snow pours forth, the hill man constantly adjusts the direction of the spray to assure a smooth cover. Heavy buildups of snow are spread in all high traffic areas, at the top of the slope, for instance. Areas with rope tows and similar lift systems often stockpile snow on each side of the lift track, so it easily can be moved into place when needed.

The crew foreman checks the quality of the snow too. He also keeps alert

much as half a million dollars in some cases. But manufacturers of the equipment convinced owners it was more expensive to go through a winter in which there was a dearth of snow.

Most operators in the northeastern corner of the United States now consider snow-making equipment as vital to their operations as hot coffee and ample parking. "We installed equipment to improve skiing during the early and late seasons," says Sepp Ruschp, head of the Mount Mansfield Company, which operates the Spruce Peak and Mount Mansfield ski areas in Verfor any drop in nozzle pressure, an indication that the waterline or the gun may be freezing up. If a freeze-up does occur, the line must be blown out or the gun thawed.

At one New York ski area, the snow-making guns are mounted atop thirty-foot towers, which enables each one to spread snow over an extremely wide area. The direction in which each gun points is controlled by ropes.

Snow is also a problem for those ski areas which are blessed with it in abundance. Seldom is snow just right for skiing as it falls from the sky, so work crews must be sent out to groom the slopes after every storm. Powdery snow has to be packed. Drifts must be mashed flat. Bare spots have to be covered. Crusted snow and ice have to be crushed fine.

Every ski area must purchase an impressive array of expensive over-snow vehicles to do this pampering. The basic piece of equipment is a bulldozer-like vehicle called a "crawler." It is equipped with heavy metal tracks almost a yard wide that enable the machine to climb the steepest slopes. Because they are so wide, the tracks also act to spread the weight of the crawler over a large area, preventing the vehicle from packing down the snow.

Many ski areas groom their snow every day. Crews head out onto the slopes late each afternoon and work until midnight. When the skiers awake in the morning, the slopes are ready.

The grooming tasks are varied, for the quality of the snow changes with the temperature. The amount of use the slope has received is another factor that must be considered.

Suppose a slope is powdered with six to eight inches of snow over a base of "old" snow. Then grooming involves dragging a chain mat over the slope. This operation settles the snow and leaves the mountain with an easy-to-ski surface.

If the snowfall is deeper than eight inches, a roller is towed over the snow. The roller looks like a section of corrugated culvert. It is about ten feet long and as much as 36 inches in diameter.

The roller must actually roll as it is pulled, not slide. The corrugations increase the rolling tendency. Before the roller is taken out on the slope for the

A gun lays down a thick, white snow blanket

first time each season, it is painted with liquid floor wax or melted paraffin. This prevents snow from sticking to it.

In the case of unseasonal temperatures, 28 degrees or higher, the roller is used over a light snowfall in preference to the chain mat. The warming trend causes the snow to become sticky and the mat will leave lumps of snow and generally bumpy conditions behind.

A covering of deep, wet snow is rolled with what one manager calls a "flexible packer." In size and shape it is similar to the conventional roller, but the packer is covered with six inches of foam rubber padding and wrapped in a waterproof cover. This type of roller packs the snow, but not too firmly.

After a weekend or a holiday period, the snow is likely to be worn away from areas where the traffic has been heavy. In that case it becomes the job of the mountain crew to use the big-bladed crawlers to plow snow from the sides of the slope to the center and then pack it down.

If no new snow falls over an extended period, the crew may take their crawlers into the woods adjacent to the slopes and trails, and plow snow out. But in order to perform this operation, the wooded area must previously have been cleared of rocks, stumps, and undergrowth. Otherwise, these will be pushed out on to the slope with the snow.

Man-made snow has to be groomed too. Natural snow is made of intricately branched icy crystals which, in quantity, produce a powdery condition, but artificial snow is composed of tiny droplets of ice. This means that man-made snow packs more readily and turns to ice faster. It has to be harrowed to keep it fluffed up. This involves dragging a heavy steel frame with spikelike teeth over the slope.

Area managers treat their over-snow equipment with diligent care. A new crawler may cost as much as $10,000, but if it fails to operate when needed, it is worthless.

Every ski area with a fleet of vehicles has at least one skilled mechanic on its payroll to keep the equipment in tip-top operating condition. "And you can't allow just anyone to drive the vehicles," a New York operator points out. "You have to have careful drivers. The equipment may look rugged, but it's not, not from an operational standpoint anyway. A 'cowboy' can tear up a crawler in a matter of minutes."

The equipment has to be garaged in a heated building too. This makes it easy to repair and maintain the vehicles. It also permits the snow to melt away from the vehicle undercarriage and tracks, so the operator can inspect the principal mechanical parts.

The area's lift equipment gets just as much attention as its snow. During each skiing day, maintenance crews constantly check the lifts to prevent breakdowns. "You have to have skilled men on the job every minute," says one operator. "After all, winter is the only

Youngsters never fail to enjoy a ride on the lifts

time you have to make money. If you lose some weekend business because you have to close down a lift, it can be a serious financial loss."

There are several different types of lifts, and each one presents different maintenance problems. The simplest type of lift is the rope tow. The skier, wearing skis, takes hold of the rope and is hauled up the hill. The J-bar lift has a rigid seat, and the T-bar is shaped like an anchor with a double seat.

Many areas have chair lifts. The chairs resemble benches, and seat two, three, or four skiers at a time. Each chair is suspended from a cable supported by a series of towers. Once seated, the skiers are carried majestically to the mountaintop.

The gondola is the most luxurious of

lifts. The skiers ride aloft in small groups enclosed in plastic pods. They are protected from the cold weather or wind.

In the case of rope tows, maintenance crews have to plow out the rope track whenever necessary. The tow gears have to be lubricated, and the lift's braking mechanism has to be checked frequently.

Each year lift equipment becomes more splendid, and many observers have predicted that the simple rope tow is headed for extinction. Yet many area operators continue to favor the rope tow over other lifts.

Rope tows represent the least expensive form of uphill transport, and they are easy to operate and maintain. The new ropes with synthetic fibers are a great boon. Hemp ropes used to twist, causing breakdowns, but the synthetics resist twisting.

Another reason some ski area operators favor the rope tow is that it can be installed on the most rugged of slopes, over ridges and knobs, if necessary. Often it is not economical to install a cable lift over rugged terrain.

Tow lifts can be short or long. Caberfae ski area near Cadillac, Michigan, has a beginner's slope that is serviced by a rope tow only 150 feet long. It is one of the sixteen rope tows scattered about Caberfae's 580 acres of slopes. The area operates chair lifts too.

"Most of our customers prefer the rope tows because they're part of the action here," says Merle Trapp, manager of Caberfae. "Kids especially like them because they go up a hill almost as fast as they come down."

One problem with rope tows is that the ropes themselves sometimes ice up. There is nothing pleasant about grabbing an icy rope on a subfreezing day, and skiers complain. But rope tow experts claim that icing only occurs when the uphill rope touches the ground at some point. If the tow track is carefully contoured to match the slope, this won't happen.

When checking on a chair lift, members of the maintenance team ride the lift and inspect the alignment of the sheaves, the grooved rimmed wheels that hold the lift cable. Misalignment of the sheaves, sometimes caused by a sudden shift in temperature, can cause a breakdown. Sheaves are adjustable and it is not difficult to bring one back

Nowadays, ski areas must appeal to family groups

into line if the trouble is spotted right away.

If the cable is making a scraping noise as it passes through the sheave, it indicates that the rubber sheave liner is worn. The crew replaces the sheave when the lift closes down at night.

Not too many years ago, skiing was regarded as an adults-only sport, but today many ski areas have been almost taken over by family groups. Many area operators seek to attract family business by offering reduced-price accommodations to families with children. Nurseries for toddlers are common now.

The family invasion created some problems for ski area operators. Special slopes had to be set aside for the youngsters. Special tows, usually simple rope tows, had to be erected. Instruction classes for the young novice skier had to be introduced, and rental shops had to be stocked with boots, skis, and poles in junior sizes. "You have to cater to the family skier with children nowadays," says one area owner. "If you don't, you might as well turn the place over to a real estate developer."

With so many newcomers being attracted to the sport, many areas have put an emphasis on skiing instruction.

Sometimes the director of the ski school will be a "name" skier, perhaps a former national champion. "But skiing ability and national renown aren't the most important factors in selecting a ski school director and his instructors," says the manager of a Vermont area. "Appearance is a principal consideration. We expect all our school personnel to be attractive in appearance and well-groomed.

"Of course, the instructors have to be excellent skiers, but we rate teaching ability ahead of skiing skill. Many students are nervous and tense when they turn out for skiing instruction. But a capable instructor has the ability to put students at ease, and he helps them gain in confidence day by day, even as the challenges increase.

"An instructor has to be able to demonstrate ski technique, and also be able to imitate his students' mistakes. This gives each student a clear idea of what he or she is doing wrong."

At some ski areas, skiing instruction includes a school skiing program. Boys and girls from local schools are bussed to the area one afternoon a week for several weeks for on-the-slope lessons.

It is not easy to get a school skiing program started. The first step is to get school administrators to support the idea. "This is often the toughest part of the job," says the owner of a west-

Ski instructors are selected for their teaching skill; their ability as skiers is secondary

ern Massachusetts ski area. "When you say 'skiing' to a school principal, he right away gets a picture of kids on crutches.

"You have to be ready to stress the safety aspects of the program, and the fact that no one starts out at the top of the mountain. The kids learn step by step. I also emphasize the physical fitness aspects of skiing, the fact that it's terrific exercise, and it's a sport a person can enjoy throughout his lifetime."

Once the school administration approves the idea, the organizational work begins. Arrangements have to be made for bus transportation to and from the slope. Instructors have to be hired. The boys and girls have to be signed up.

Virtually all areas with school skiing programs charge the youngsters an instruction fee. "The fee is important," says one operator. "It not only helps us to pay our expenses, but the kids are more serious, more attentive when they have to pay."

One of the country's most successful school skiing programs is conducted by the Mt. Tom ski area in Holyoke, Massachusetts. It draws pupils from thirty-five high schools, prep schools, and colleges for its six-week program. More than five thousand boys and girls received ski instruction at Mt. Tom during one recent season.

School skiing never fails to appeal to the students. A school program conducted at the Dodge Ridge, California, ski area has proved so popular that schools in the region have had to restrict the program to those students with better-than-average grades. You have to have a "B—" average to be eligible.

Some youngsters became surprisingly skilled after just a few lessons. "The trick is to bring them along slowly," says one instructor. "We begin by explaining the etiquette of skiing and some safety precautions, like how to fall. We teach them to go down easily, never to 'fight' a fall.

"Then we go into the fundamentals —walking on skis and climbing a gentle slope. Each pupil must get the 'feel' of his skis before he's allowed to try a rope tow."

Most ski schools allow youngsters to set their own pace. Some pupils leave the novice stage almost immediately, and are ready to try "straight running," that is, a downhill descent, after only two or three lessons. The next step is to teach the student to brake his descent by means of the "snowplow," a maneuver in which the tails of the skis are pushed out. The V position of the skis acts as a plow, first slowing and then stopping the skier.

The students with the most ability are taught how to make downhill turns. Some even learn to ski parallel, that is skiing with the skis together while turning. This is one of the most advanced forms of the skiing art.

"Youngsters learn quickly," says Neil Robinson, who supervises the ski school operation at the Glen Ellen, Vermont, ski area. "In fact, they are often easier to teach than some adults. Kids are natural mimics. Show them how to do something, and they're able to imitate the action almost perfectly. That's why they're easy to teach."

Skiing can be a hazardous sport. A skier who tries a slope beyond his skill (the foremost cause of skiing accidents) may twist or tear a muscle or fracture a limb. Cuts and sprains are not exactly uncommon.

But every ski area has an accident prevention program. It involves marking slopes and trails as to their degree of difficulty, and posting maps of the ski area.

The ski area manager also seeks to develop an efficient corps of ski patrolmen. They are the policemen of the slopes, enforcing traffic regulations. They are also specialists in giving aid to injured skiers.

A ski area usually has at least one full-time patrolman as member of its staff. The other patrolmen, and there may be dozens of them, are all volunteers, members of the National Ski Patrol System. The area manager sees to it that they are supplied with the proper equipment, including first-aid supplies, blankets, and toboggans, which are necessary in carrying injured skiers from the slopes.

To most of the country's six million skiers, the sport is almost as seasonal as Christmas. But running a ski area is a year-round operation.

Almost as soon as the last lift engine stops churning, maintenance crews set to work preparing for the season to

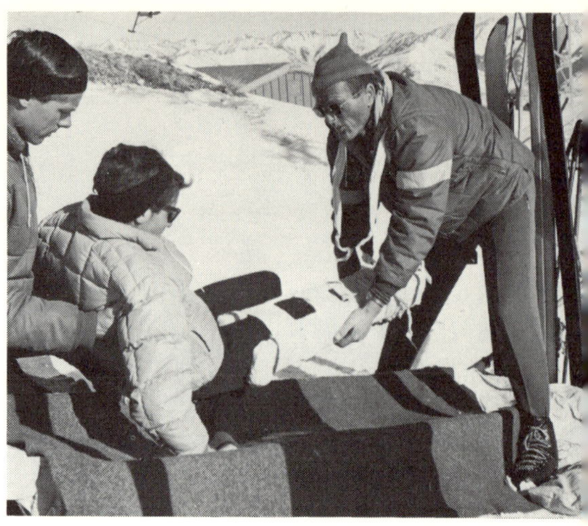

Experienced ski patrolmen are vital to the operation of every ski area

come. "Operation Get Ready" begins with a careful inventory of all equipment and supplies, all parts and fuels. This enables the area manager to get a clear idea of his costs over the previous season. It also helps him in ordering for the season ahead.

The next step is to haul all movable equipment down from the mountain and store it away. This includes such items as snow fences, portable telephone booths, first-aid stations, and toboggans.

If this equipment were left on the mountain during the spring and summer, it would soon become weatherbeaten or it might be stolen. And there is one other reason for storing it away —porcupines. Many resorts in Vermont and New Hampshire report that these quilled vandals nibble away at almost any equipment they can find.

At Mad River, Vermont, porcupines spent a good part of one summer chewing on several wooden huts used by slope attendants. Employees thwarted the mischief-makers by sheathing the huts with sheets of tin. Porcupines at Mad River also climbed the lift poles to nibble away at the rubber sheave liners and did about $2,000 worth of damage. To prevent more, the maintenance crew installed large tin disks about halfway up each lift pole. The porcupines could not climb beyond the disks.

All lift equipment is carefully inspected during the summer. In the case of rope tows, the gears must be greased and the ropes inspected for wear. Rope maintenance is a good deal easier since ropes of synthetic materials have replaced hemp. The synthetic ropes can last three seasons, where hemp ropes were likely to wear out after only one season of use.

"And it doesn't hurt synthetic ropes if you leave them out all summer," says a New Hampshire area operator. "But you have to suspend the ropes above ground. If you don't, rodents gnaw away at them. Field mice consider some synthetic fibers to be a delicacy."

Chair or gondola lifts are disassembled and worn parts replaced. Sheaves are inspected for wear. The lift towers and their concrete bases are checked for cracks that might indicate weakening. The bull wheel, the main driving wheel that transmits power from the lift engine to the cable, may have to be overhauled.

The lift cable gets a careful examination over its entire length. If any worn areas or broken strands are found, the manager may call in a wire rope engineer. He decides whether the worn section should be cut out of the cable and sent to a laboratory for analysis. The tests performed there tell whether a new cable section must be purchased.

The lift engines and snow-making machinery receive a thorough going-over. Sometimes it is necessary to call in a diesel mechanic to restore the lift machinery to first-class operating condition.

At the same time the mechanical equipment is being overhauled, other maintenance crews are at work on the ski trails. They first inspect all trails for "washouts." Sections of the trails that show the slightest sign of erosion are marked for repair. Later they will be graded and planted with grass seed.

Healthy turf, by binding the soil together, helps to prevent erosion. Any bare spot on the trails is raked, fertilized, and seeded. At many areas, maintenance crews scatter hay along the trails to serve as a cushion for early snow.

The base lodge and the base area in general have to be put in readiness too. Directional signs and bulletin boards have to be repainted. Booths have to be made ready for the sale of lift tickets, and the tickets themselves must be ordered. The base lodge may need painting and some repair work.

It is usually the responsibility of the area manager to ready the ski shop, where equipment is purchased and rented, for opening day. This may involve ordering skis, boots, poles, and other necessary equipment and supplies.

During the early weeks of the fall, a good part of the manager's time will be given over to interviewing and hiring part-time employees, people who will assist the full-time staff once the season opens. Each ticket seller, parking lot attendant, waiter, and waitress must be carefully selected, for each is in almost constant contact with the public. "Our customers think of us in terms of our staff members," one manager says. "One rude employee can do us more harm than a lift breakdown."

Courtesy is also a necessity on the part of lift men, the attendants who help skiers on and off lift equipment. "A lift attendant may have twenty or more opportunities to make a favorable impression on a customer," one area manager points out. "A good lift man is a real asset, but one who doesn't know his job or is rude can seriously harm your business."

Except for the maintenance work that goes on, most ski areas close down

Beginners first learn to walk on skis, then climb a gentle slope

42

during much of the spring and fall and throughout the summer. But there are a growing number that are beginning to operate on a year-round basis. Instead of from skiers, the business comes from conventioneers.

When holding meetings, business and professional groups need lodging for group members, dining facilities, and conference rooms. The ski resort in summertime can suit perfectly.

"I'm convinced we have just begun what could be an important part of the ski area business in the future," says a Park City, Utah, operator. "The meeting and convention business is available and just waiting to be tapped."

Kissing Bridge, near Buffalo, New York, is another ski area that seeks out convention business. The area's lodge facilities are filled each year from June through October. "Off-season business amounts to about one third of our yearly income," says the president of the Kissing Bridge Corporation.

Many of the larger resorts attempt to attract not only men attending meetings or conventions but also their families. At Manor Vail, Colorado, most groups include wives and children. During the day, the wives go shopping or enjoy the area's off-season recreational facilities, which include swimming, golf, and tennis. Sun Valley has named May, June, September, and October as convention months, and the mammoth resort plays host to about 120 meetings and conventions each year.

Another summertime task for the ski area manager is to plan his promotion and advertising for the months ahead. He supervises the preparation of the colorful brochures that proclaim the wonders of his resort, and decides how much money to budget for advertising and where the money will be spent. He is likely to address local business clubs and social groups to stir up interest in the area, and he assigns his ski school director to contact local high schools and prep schools to arrange skiing programs for students.

Early in the fall, all movable gear is taken from storage and hauled back up the mountain. The lift machinery and snow-making equipment get a final inspection. Operation Get Ready is over. The area manager begins to search the sky for those big, fluffy, and menacing clouds that mean snow—and the sound of jingling cash registers.

4

RESTAURANT

"WHAT'S THE 'SECRET' of a successful restaurant?" someone once asked Bruno Benarbo, managing director of New York City's Mamma Leone's, one of the most popular and prosperous restaurants in the United States. Mamma Leone's may serve as many as 4,000 dinners on a Saturday night, and its annual gross income approaches $1,000,000, figures that add up to real soaring success.

Mr. Benarbo didn't hesitate in answering the question. "Food is number one," he said. "You must serve good food.

"Service is second. The waiters must be courteous and efficient.

"The restaurant site is important too. You have to have a location that's convenient to the type of people you expect to attract.

"When you have all these, then it's important to make your guests feel welcome," said Mr. Benarbo. "Even more than that, you have to make them feel like they're taking part in a celebration, make them feel like it's New Year's Eve. If there is one 'secret' in the operation of a successful restaurant, that's it."

When you approach Mamma Leone's, you notice that the exterior is brightly lit. The doorman greets you warmly. As you pass into the restaurant, a hostess dressed in a traditional Italian costume approaches your party. Smiling, she says, "*Buona sera*" (Good evening). The maître d' bows when he greets your party, and then a host escorts you to your table. All of this goes toward making you feel "like it's New Year's Eve."

Mamma Leone's represents one of the country's 367,000 individual eating establishments, a tiny segment of the giant food service industry. According to the National Restaurant Association, annual sales total $30 billion, making the industry the third largest in the United States.

Experts recognize three different types of restaurants. First, there are the specialty restaurants, those which serve only one or two particular types of food. Typical of these are the fried chicken and French fries stands, hamburger houses, pancake and waffle shops, and clam bars.

The number of specialty restaurants has multiplied dramatically in recent years. They are usually franchise operations. This means that a statewide or nationwide chain licenses a restaurant operator to sell its products within a specified area. For this privilege, the operator agrees to buy all equipment and supplies from the parent company or he agrees to pay the parent company a commission on restaurant sales.

While your choice of food items is severely limited when you dine at a specialty restaurant, the food that is served is likely to be quite toothsome. The fried chicken is crisp and tasty. The doughnuts are fresh and feather-light, and come in twenty-nine different varieties. The hamburgers are full-flavored and juicy, and served with a savory sauce. And the prices at a specialty restaurant are every bit as appealing as the food. Items like the 19-cent milkshake and the 29-cent roast beef sandwich on a sesame roll enable the customer to satisfy his hunger at a budget price.

A convenient location is another hallmark of specialty restaurants. You see them on well-traveled highways, usually on the outskirts of cities. There are always ample parking facilities.

A second type of restaurant is the "short-order" restaurant. *Quick*-order restaurant might be a more appropriate term, for operations of this type are noted for the speed with which they prepare easy-to-make snacks and meals.

Hamburgers, bacon and eggs, hot and cold sandwiches of every type, and "platters"—complete meals served on a single dish—are standard fare in the short-order restaurant. Diners, snack bars, luncheonettes, and most drive-ins are included in this category.

Often the short-order restaurant is located in a downtown area, and it does most of its business at lunchtime. The average check is not large, so the short-order restaurant must depend on quick turnover. Every seat must be occupied several times during the lunch period. This means the help has to be quick and efficient, and most hot meals have to be prepared in advance.

The third type of restaurant, and the one this chapter focuses upon, is the table service restaurant. Here the food is prepared to the customers' tastes, and all food and beverages are served by waiters or waitresses. The hospitable attitude displayed by everyone from the hatcheck girl to the maître d', the attractive decor, and the delectable meal itself—all of these contribute toward making the meal in a well-run table service restaurant an exciting experience.

The operation of almost every large restaurant is divided into three areas —the kitchen and food preparation, the dining room and food service, and control and management. All three of these departments are supervised by the restaurant manager.

An executive chef heads the food service department. Along with the general manager and the controller, the

The restaurant's food service department is headed by an executive chef

executive chef plans the restaurant's menus, a responsibility that involves forecasting the number of guests expected each evening, and pricing the menu items for that evening. But the head chef's main responsibilities are in the kitchen, where he supervises the preparation of all food.

He tests cooked foods by tasting or smelling them, and he inspects portions to see that they are of proper size. Many different types of cooks may work for the head chef. They include a roast or meat cook, vegetable cook, soup cook, sauce cook, and pastry chef.

At a smaller restaurant, the kitchen staff may be made up of only a handful of cooks, with each having a wide assortment of duties. A cook's day may begin in the predawn hours when he enters the dark, empty restaurant to light his ranges, ovens, and the *bain-marie,* a large metal container with hot-water-heated compartments to keep food warm. He unlocks the refrigerators and storerooms.

If the restaurant serves breakfast, the cook prepares bacon, scrambled eggs, and hot cereals. These items are usually cooked in advance and placed in pans or large bowls ready for service. The cook also prepares soup stock, the liquid base from which soup is made, and he weighs out the vegetables that will be used in making the soups.

All the while, he is preparing other foods as they are ordered. A night cook has prepared the roasts, but the day cook must deep-fry or bake fish, broil steaks or chops, and cook vegetables.

Before his day ends, the day cook will select the recipe cards from the restaurant's file to be used for preparing the following day's menu. He removes roasts from the refrigerator for the cook who is to follow him on duty, and he may pre-prepare some of the foods for the next day's menu.

Through the day, the cook works constantly to keep his work area clean and well-ordered. He cleans the chopper, slicer, or mixer after using them. He cleans all his kitchen utensils and returns them to storage. When the next cook takes over, everything is in readiness.

A pastry cook has a much different set of duties. It is his job to prepare almost all the restaurant's fancy baked goods, including cakes, pies, puddings, shortcake, biscuits, and cheesecakes. He may bake specialty breads, such as corn bread and brown bread. He may also prepare cooked fruit, like prunes or rhubarb, and bake dessert apples. If the restaurant serves breakfast, the pastry chef is the one who mixes up the pancake batter used by the griddle cook, and he bakes muffins, hot breads, and other pastries for breakfast service.

The serving of food in a large restaurant is directed by the dining room supervisor. The employees in his department include the host or hostess, the cashier, the food checker, the waiters, and the busboys. Of all of these, the waiters are the most important. It is the waiters who represent the restaurant to the patrons. The success or failure of an establishment can depend on the type of service they give.

Basically, the waiter takes the order and serves the food. The job seems simple, but it is not.

The waiter's responsibility begins before the guests arrive. He must inspect the table to see that it is properly set, and be certain that the linen, silver, and china are perfectly clean.

The waiter has to have full knowledge of all the food items on the menu, and be able to describe all dishes. When a patron asks, "What is veal scallopine?" the waiter has to be able to answer that it is thin, flattened-out slices of veal, flavored with wine and cooked in butter. Some dishes, like the dramatically fiery dessert cherries jubilee, may require special serving techniques, and the waiter must know them too.

But these are only the mechanics of the job. More than anything else, the waiter must display an attitude of genuine hospitality. He must do all he can to make guests feel welcome.

Besides being friendly and having a pleasant smile, there is much a waiter can do to add to the patrons' enjoyment of the meal. He can bring them more water as they need it, extra rolls and butter, and more coffee. Picking up a napkin and replacing it with a fresh one, "crumbing" (removing crumbs from) the table between courses—these are the niceties that customers appreciate.

"A waiter," says a New England restaurant waiter, "may have some failing when it comes to serving food, but he can still be a good waiter, just so long as he maintains a cheerful disposition and shows that he wants to please. Most people will put up with an occasional boner in service, but they will not stand for a waiter who is unpleasant or the least bit surly."

While the restaurant operator has little control over what he must pay his wholesalers for the various food items he purchases, there is much he can do in the handling of food merchandise to keep those costs at a minimum. For example, when food is delivered he must resist the temptation to accept it quickly and send the deliveryman on his way.

"Just as you count your change at a bank teller's window, you must check your food when it is delivered," advises Paul Fairbook, a well-known expert in the food service field. The restaurant owner must weigh all meats that are delivered and count all packaged items. Any discrepancy between what has been ordered and what has been delivered must be noted on the invoice that accompanies the delivery. Later the wholesaler must be made to make an adjustment.

Refrigerated meat cuts bristle with inventory tags

Spoilage can skyrocket food costs, and special care must be made to store all food properly. Any perishables must be placed in refrigerators or freezers immediately. All storerooms must have secure locks.

The proper handling of food deliveries is only one small part of every restaurant's control setup. "It's difficult to be successful in the restaurant business today without rigid bookkeeping," says Michael Barrera, a group controller for Restaurant Associates, Inc., of New York City. "Proper controls help prevent overordering. Controls cut down on wasteful practices by the kitchen help. They indicate whether your restaurant is adequately staffed, or perhaps overstaffed. And controls help prevent pilferage and outright theft on the part of dishonest employees."

A small restaurant is likely to use the services of an accountant in setting up a control system, but a large food-serving operation will employ a full-time food and beverage controller. He is a keyman in the restaurant's operation. His judgment is considered in planning portion sizes and recipes. He advises on food and beverage purchases. He establishes the systems used in receiving food and beverages from the storeroom. He takes periodic inventories of all food and beverage items to check the accuracy of his records.

Under the system he establishes, food is issued only on the basis of a written order, which must be signed by the head chef or an authorized assistant. And recipes are standardized. The days of the chef who prepared his specialties by following "secret" recipes have gone the way of the five-cent candy bar. Today each recipe must be carefully tested and then the cost determined to the penny. Cooks must follow a standard set of instructions in preparing dishes, and cooking methods have to be the same each time the dish is prepared.

48

Cash register controls are also vital. Every restaurant has to have some method of keeping track of the money that is received. Most cash registers tabulate the money rung up, and this serves as a check.

But suppose a dishonest waiter pockets money he collects from a patron for food. The money never reaches the register to be tabulated. How is this prevented? Most restaurants use a system of duplicate checks. When a waiter writes your order on a check, he is also writing a carbon duplicate. The duplicate is given to the cook and serves as a written order for him to prepare the meal.

The original is given to the cashier. Using a printing cash register, the cashier prepares an itemized check for each table. When your party has finished the meal, the waiter obtains the check from the cashier, who expects him to return with the total amount due.

A dishonest waiter could defeat this system by not writing a check for the ordered food. He could, for example, slip a dessert out of the kitchen, serve it to you, charge you for it, and then pocket the money. Since the item did not appear on any check, the cashier would have no knowledge of the order. This is why all large restaurants have food checkers. Stationed in an area between the kitchen and the dining room through which waiters must pass, the checker notes each item that leaves the kitchen to be certain a check has been written for it.

Setting prices is a delicate art in the restaurant business. The price the restaurant patron is charged for a meal must take into consideration the cost of the food and the amount of labor that has gone into its preparation. But these are only the basic items. The restaurant owner must also take into account the prices being charged at restaurants similar to his. He will be inviting customer resistance if he charges prices much higher than those of the competition.

More and more restaurant owners are limiting the number of items they offer. It is not difficult to understand why. It simplifies every phase of the operation—food purchasing, preparation, and serving. A short menu means cost control is easier too.

"I've found my customers would prefer to make their selection from a relatively few items," says the owner of a Chicago restaurant. "They don't want to wrestle with a menu that's the size of a tabloid newspaper. They're here to relax."

The menu, of course, is the restaurant's basic sales tool, and owners devote long hours toward planning menu style and appearance. An exclusive gourmet restaurant may not have any menu at all. Patrons reach a decision after conferring with the maître d'. But this is the exception. The usual practice is to offer a menu that is both distinctive and distinguished.

An exclusive Worcester, Massachusetts, restaurant, which serves meals in the Yankee tradition, presents menus

Specialty restaurants are often operated under the names of well-known sports or entertainment figures

that are made to resemble parchment scrolls. A restaurant operated by former boxing champion Rocky Graziano features a menu in the shape of a boxing glove.

Many of the country's leading restaurants have their menus printed daily. This enables them to make last-minute price changes. They can also list special dishes without having to resort to "clip-ons," those small one-page attachments that are fixed to the menu pages of popular-priced restaurants. No fashionable restaurant would ever use a clip-on. Some restaurants encourage patrons to take their menus home with them. The menu then serves as an inexpensive form of advertising.

Many leading restaurants advertise in local daily newspapers in an effort to win new customers. Restaurants also stage special "nights" to build their business. For example, on an "Italian Night," Italian cuisine is featured; waiters wear gondoliers' outfits, and strolling mandolin players entertain. On a "Western Night" tables and chairs are moved outdoors. Meat dishes are barbecued on charcoal grills, and patrons dine by torchlight. A cowboy band provides music.

Restaurant managers plan diligently to make such occasions as festive as possible. "You have to create a party atmosphere," says a Midwest restaurateur. "We always give away favors to the women guests. Special costumes and special lighting, lanterns or torches or something, are important, and special music is as necessary as food and drink.

"Then you have to go to work and advertise and publicize the event. We send mailings to our regular customers and instruct our employees to 'talk it up.' We promote the event in the local newspaper. Planning and selling the affair make the difference between its success or failure."

At Christmas, at New Year's, and Easter, Mamma Leone's takes on a carnival atmosphere. The management strings a dazzling display of lights, serves special dishes, and fills the renowned restaurant with lively music.

A table piled high with appetizing food awaits restaurant guests

But perhaps the biggest celebration of all at Mamma Leone's is "Carnevale," a roaring fiesta with a rich history. Italians of long ago felt that a period of celebration was needed to counterbalance the fasting and self-denial of Lent. So in the week before Ash Wednesday, the day Lent begins, great feasts of food and music were held throughout Italy, with each town trying to outdo the other. If one village had a banquet every day for seven days, the neighboring village would have *two* banquets every day. Mamma Leone's version of "Carnevale" is meant to capture the Old World flavor of the celebration.

Often a restaurant's promotion efforts take the form of "extras" in the way of food or service. A Chicago restaurant offers patrons home-baked bread, "with loads of butter," a wide array of relishes from a rolling cart, unlimited coffee, and allows patrons to mix their own salads, providing a special mixing table for the purpose. The table is piled high with lettuce, cucumbers, tomatoes, and an assortment of garnishes.

At Mamma Leone's, when you are shown to your table, an "extra" is immediately apparent. An appealing dish of celery, olives, tomatoes, green peppers, scallions, plus a hefty wedge of Swiss cheese are waiting to be devoured. "To us," says Bruno Benarbo, "nothing could be worse than showing guests to an empty table. Having food already there adds to the festive nature of the meal."

Extras can also take the form of

Free stagecoach rides for youngsters is the way one New York restaurant promotes its business

51

Window decals advertise a restaurant's credit card memberships

special table decorations, even fresh-cut flowers. Additional services also include the gift cake for a birthday party, the mints or candies served after dessert, or distinctively designed tableware. All these devices represent efforts by the restaurant to make your meal something special, to make you want to return. Sometimes such planning is subtle, as when the restaurant serves milk in an amber-colored glass to make it appear creamier, or uses smaller-than-normal plates to make the portions seem larger.

Often a restaurant will serve regional dishes to attract patronage. Most Boston restaurants feature broiled live lobster. In southern California, a restaurant menu is likely to feature abalone, the meat of large snails found in California coastal waters. In Baltimore, it is crab cakes. There are countless other examples.

Credit cards have become important in the operation of a successful restaurant. Almost every restaurant subscribes to one or more of the national credit card companies. This enables the restaurant to attract businessmen who charge their meals. But this benefit costs. The restaurant must pay 3 to 7 percent of the amount of the check to the credit card organization.

Some restaurants issue their own personal credit cards, valid only when dining in their restaurant. Of course, this policy involves the restaurant owner in keeping accounts and billing.

Restaurant owners use many other ways to attract customers. But owners agree that winning new customers is not nearly as important as satisfying present ones. This means the restaurant must serve good food, and courtesy and efficiency must keynote the conduct of the restaurant staff. The meal must become a pleasant memory.

"Thank you for coming," the waiter says as you leave the table. "Good night, sir," says the doorman. "Come back and see us soon." If it is a well-run restaurant, you will.

5

SUMMER CAMP

Every camp director would like the boys and girls in his charge to write home letters like this one. If the camp is well run, they are quite likely to.

A camp that is operated thoughtfully and efficiently becomes, to quote the director of a large western Massachusetts camp, "a child's world." Every activity must be directed toward that goal.

The American Camping Association, a nationwide organization composed of camp owners, directors, and counselors, credits Frederick William Gunn, the founder of the Gunnery School for Boys in Washington, Connecticut, as one of the leaders in the development of organized camping in the United States. In 1861, Gunn and his wife led the school's student body on a camping expedition to Milford-on-the-Sound, Connecticut, for a two-week stay. The excursion was so successful that camping was established as a permanent fixture on the school curriculum.

A few privately operated camps were established during the latter part of the nineteenth century, but the real moving force in the growth of organized camping came a few decades later from such organizations as the Young Men's Christian Association (the Y.M.C.A.) and the Boy Scouts of America. The Girl Scouts of the U.S.A., the Camp Fire Girls, and the Young Women's Christian Association (the Y.W.C.A.) were other organizations that spearheaded camping interest.

Camping has come a long way since the days of Mr. Gunn and his Gunnery School campers. Today, according to the American Camping Association, there are approximately 8,000 resident camps and 2,600 day camps in operation. About 8,000,000 boys and girls enjoy the benefits of camping each year.

Camps cover a wide range of types.

Some differ according to the organization that sponsors the camp. Besides the organizations mentioned above, camps are operated by the American Red Cross, Big Brothers of America, 4-H Clubs, Catholic Youth Organization, Young Men's and Young Women's Hebrew Association, The Salvation Army, and Volunteers of America, Inc. There are camps sponsored by labor unions, city recreation departments, and private and municipal welfare agencies. There are church camps representing every religious denomination.

Other camps are privately operated. This means they are owned by an individual or group of individuals.

Each camp, whether an organization camp or a private camp, is run by a director, a man or woman with long experience in camping. His background is likely to include training in such subjects as education, biology, philosophy, and human relations. The success of the camp depends on the director, his ideas, and the standards he sets.

The camp director is busy twelve months a year. In January, when the campers are in school and their thoughts far from horseback riding and hiking trips, he writes to parents. "It's winter and it's cold and summer seems far away," his letter is likely to say, "but now is the time to make summer plans." He encloses an enrollment application with the letter.

It is during the winter that the camp director contacts suppliers to make arrangements for food purchases. The subject of price is settled and delivery schedules are agreed upon.

Well before spring arrives, the director has planned all out-of-camp hikes and canoe trips. He has mapped the routes and obtained permission from owners to use private property.

The director keeps in constant contact with the parents of all campers. They receive an equipment and clothing list, and also a questionnaire requesting information about their camper's hobbies, special interests, and preferences in playmates. The questionnaire asks: "Does he enjoy younger or older children or those of his own age? Does he prefer groups or to play alone?"

"The information we get from these questionnaires is extremely important to us," says one camp director. "It helps us to get to know a child more quickly, to work with him effectively, and to help him to derive the greatest reward and satisfaction from his camping stay."

During the winter and spring the director fills any openings that may exist on his staff. Many directors testify that the task of recruiting, selecting, and hiring new staff members is one of the most difficult tasks they face. A camp may boast deluxe accommodations, serve gourmet food, and offer a sports and recreation program that rivals the Olympic Games, but unless the operation is staffed with competent people, the other factors have little meaning.

*A person who works with campers must be deeply interested
in children and offer special skills and experience*

The most important staff members are the counselors because they are in almost constant contact with the campers. "Counselors are critical to your success," says the director of a New Jersey coed camp. "If a boy or a girl has a pleasant relationship with his or her counselor, then we can expect the camper to return the next summer. But if a camper and counselor don't hit it off too well, then we're not going to see that camper again."

When recruiting new counselors, the camp director looks for young men and women of high moral character and good judgment. The applicant has to show that he or she is interested in children and enthusiastic about the camp and its projects.

"It really takes a special type of person," says the director of a Pennsylvania camp, "a person able to fill a wide range of roles, that of substitute parent, friend, adviser, and instructor."

To find qualified counselors, camp directors contact colleges, technical schools, and seminaries that have counselor training programs for undergraduates. Sometimes counselors are hired from the teaching or coaching ranks.

Each prospective counselor fills out a detailed application form. Each is carefully interviewed by the camp director.

"First of all, I'm concerned about appearance," says the personnel director of a large camp outside New York City. "If we're hiring a young man, we expect him to be clean-cut. A girl must be trim and well-groomed.

"Of course, character and person-

55

ality are about equal in importance to appearance. Our young men and women counselors have to be wholesome in character, enthusiastic about their work, and emotionally mature.

"If an applicant meets our standards as far as these requirements are concerned, then we look into his or her educational background and try to learn about any special skills he or she might have.

"We're also concerned about the work experience any prospective counselor might have had, his family background, and his status as far as military service is concerned.

"A few applicants are only concerned with how much money they're going to earn, or how many nights a week they're going to be free from work. These people don't get hired. Basically, we try to find young men and women who will regard the children and the children's interest with the uppermost importance."

Besides the counselors, the director hires the supervisors for each one of the camp's activities—swimming, sailing, games, handicrafts, and all the others. Often the same supervisors return to the same camps each year, but when openings do occur the director must find new people with the necessary skill and experience.

A nurse and a doctor must be hired. Large camps also employ a business manager whose job it is to receive the campers' tuition fees, pay the camp bills, and in general, keep all the camp's financial records. At some camps, the business manager supervises the buying of food and any items of equipment the camp requires.

Good food is as important to the success of a camp as sunny weather. Meals have to be skillfully prepared, attractively served, and planned with an eye toward nutritional values. The staff of a large camp includes a dietitian to plan meals, and cooks and their assistants to prepare them.

Camp menus are simple and offer frequently foods children like, such as hamburgers, pancakes, and fruit juices. But occasionally a food item is served that is not popular with children. Liver is an example. Foods of this type are included on camp menus for their nutritional value.

Most directors plan menus about

Camp swimming programs demand a qualified instructor

Good food is as important to the operation of a camp as sunny weather

two weeks in advance, which enables the camp to buy the necessary food items efficiently and economically. Often the menus follow a fixed pattern that is repeated every three days, with slight changes in the menu items. For example, a dinner menu might follow this three-meal pattern:

Day 1

Soup
Salad
Sandwich on whole wheat bread
Fruit dessert
Milk

Day 2

Egg, cheese, or fish main dish
Salad
Bread and butter
Pudding
Milk

Day 3

Meat main dish
Vegetable side dish
Bread and butter
Cake or cookies
Milk

How much it costs to feed children depends to some degree on their age. Experts on group feeding state that it costs about ten cents more a day to feed children ten to twelve years old than to feed youngsters seven to nine years old. Boys in their late teens, because they are growing and very active, are more expensive to feed than adults.

Most camps follow one of two methods of serving food. Some prefer "family style" service. The food is brought from the kitchen in large serving dishes. Then the counselor at each table serves portions onto each camper's plate.

In the case of food that is not to the camper's liking, he or she is usually allowed to request a small serving, but most camps expect every camper to eat at least a small portion of every food item served.

The other method of serving food is cafeteria style. Campers carry their food to tables after being served from counters.

It is rare for a camp to serve food in the kitchen onto campers' plates. "This method usually proves to be wasteful," says a camp director. "All boys and girls aren't fond of the same foods, and so you can't serve the same size portions to everyone. Serving food family style or from a cafeteria line gives campers some freedom to exercise their individual likes and dislikes."

More and more camps are using disposable tableware. Small bowls, dinner plates, and large platters of pressed and treated pulpwood, and plastic, knives, forks, spoons, and cups are preferred to conventional types of tableware for hygienic reasons.

In addition, many directors have found throwaway tableware to be more economical than china dishes and glass tumblers, which must be washed after every meal. Disposable tableware costs about 3½ cents per camper per meal. But the camp saves on the cost of the electricity to run the machine that washes the dishes, and perhaps on the initial cost of the machine itself. There is also a saving in the cost of soaps and detergents. And, most important, throwaway dishes represent a saving in the salaries of the one or more employees involved in dishwashing.

Many camps use a purchase-order system when ordering food and other supplies. A purchase order is a written request to a vendor to deliver specified goods. It always bears the signature of the camp director or his authorized representative.

One original copy of the purchase order and three carbon copies are prepared. The original copy goes to the supplier. It serves as his written direction to deliver the items requested. The quantity and price of each item is listed.

One carbon copy of the purchase order is retained by the person or department to use the goods being purchased. A copy of the purchase order for food items would be retained by the chief cook. When the goods are delivered, the cook uses his copy of the order as a check to be sure he has received every item.

A second copy goes to the camp bookkeeper. When he receives a bill from the vendor for the ordered items, he checks the bill against the purchase order to make certain they agree. The bookkeeper never pays for any goods unless he has a purchase order for them.

The third carbon copy of the purchase order goes to the camp's accounting department. By keeping track of every purchase order, the accounting department is able to maintain control of the camp finances.

Each day during the camping season the director has to be watchful that camp health policies are carried out. Refuse has to be removed from the campsite daily. Campers are often held responsible for "policing" the grounds near their cabins.

In all matters concerning sanitation, the camp must comply with health regulations established by state and county. Most states conduct an annual inspection of the camp water supply and sewage disposal facilities before granting the camp a license to operate for the season.

The camp's health program extends to each and every camper. The American Camping Association recommends that each boy or girl undergo a physical examination by his family physician, and the physician provides the camp with a certificate attesting to the camper's good health before he is accepted.

When the camper arrives, he is examined by the camp doctor or nurse, who has at hand the report from the camper's family physician. The camper's counselor is notified if any limitation must be placed on the young man's activities for reasons of health.

The camp doctor or nurse must be available twenty-four hours a day. A camper may fall and suffer a cut or bruise or break a limb. There are sunburn cases to be treated, and what camp is completely free of poison ivy and stinging insects? Each camp has an infirmary, well-stocked with first-aid supplies to meet any emergency.

A person with medical training must be available to campers 24 hours a day

Daily health inspections for each camper, usually conducted following the morning flag-raising, are also part of the camp's health program.

Not all campers' ills are physical ones. Homesickness is another problem directors must be prepared to face. "The word 'homesick' is really somewhat misleading," says the director of a New England camp for preteen girls. "Children who are away from home for the first time, and those who come to camp unaccompanied by a friend or relative, may get lonely. It's not homesickness they suffer from; it's loneliness.

"The camper is more likely to feel lonely during his or her first few days in camp, and often the condition is aggravated by nightfall. But once a camper gets used to his surroundings and makes a few friends, this feeling of depression melts away."

Camp directors and counselors are aware that being lonely may be a problem for more than a few of their campers, and they meet the problem by receiving each camper warmly and having a full schedule of activities for them. Keeping campers busy is important. "You can't give them time to think about themselves," says one camp director. "And by being involved they quickly make friendships."

Some boys and girls develop a fervent loyalty to their camp and return each year without any urging on the part of the camp management. But even these outgrow camp at last. And some are not able to return. Most camp directors must concern themselves with the problems of communication and reenrollment almost continually.

Sometimes camp directors make personal visits to parents and campers, or keep in touch with them by telephone. Other camps send campers greetings at holiday time or congratulatory messages on their birthdays. "The idea is not to let them forget you," says one director.

A T-shirt blazoned with the camp name is another popular promotion device. It serves as a reminder of the camp throughout the year.

Some camps publish small newspapers or information bulletins that are mailed to parents and campers several times a year. These tell of camp plans for the coming season, report on which counselors will be returning, and give information about the construction of new facilities or the purchase of new equipment.

Camp reunions are another tried and proven method of stimulating reenrollment and recruiting new campers. At a typical reunion, refreshments are served and motion pictures of camp activities are shown. The camp director and his staff get reacquainted with former campers and meet new prospects. Plans and projects for the season ahead are discussed.

Some camps seek to recruit new members by advertising in nationally distributed magazines. *The New York Times Magazine,* which is published every Sunday, is noted for its camp advertising. So are *Good Housekeeping, Parents' Magazine,* and *Redbook.* "Write or call," say the advertisements. A response usually brings a friendly letter, a colorful brochure, a schedule of fees, and an application form.

"When it comes to advertising, the most effective type is word-of-mouth advertising," says the director of a boys' camp in the Pocono Mountains of eastern Pennsylvania. "A camper tells his friends and schoolmates about the good time he had, and they decide to sign up with him. More important, a boy's mother will tell another mother what a terrific summer her son had. That's the way camps get most of their campers. Satisfied customers are your best salesmen."

Besides recruiting, maintenance is a

60

constant winter concern. As costs go up, some owners are trying to make maximum use of their camp facilities during the school months by renting or lending them to organized groups such as Y's, churches, or businesses. *"Use our camp* when we don't," says one advertisement. "Conferences? Workshop? Therapy Group?"

The summer camp should make the young boy or girl a healthier, happier, wiser person

In their efforts to win satisfied customers, more and more camps are becoming specialized in the activities they offer. "Modern youngsters have an enormous range of interests," says Maxwell Alexander, executive director of the Association of Private Camps, "and a camp director has to gear his program to accommodate these interests."

Swimming, baseball, basketball, and tennis, the conventional camp sports, continue to be popular, but many camps have broadened sports programs. Scuba diving and water-skiing are now the specialties at some camps.

Camp Lenox, near Lee, Massachusetts, emphasizes soccer. "It's not like baseball where you have the outfielders standing around most of the time," says the camp director. "All the kids are involved and active. Soccer is now our most popular sport."

A Dorset, Vermont, camp has a specialty of a much different type—ballet. Girls, eight to eighteen years old, come from every part of the country for seven weeks of daily ballet instruction under the direction of Marina Svetlana, once a prima ballerina of the Metropolitan Opera.

Another unusual specialty camp is Shaker Village, at Lebanon Springs, New York. Here the emphasis is on handicrafts, woodworking, and carpentry, as boys and girls work to restore old buildings once used by members of the Shaker religious sect. The youngsters also make Shaker souvenirs which are sold to aid the camp's scholarship fund. Other youngsters perform community service tasks in nearby rural villages. "The main goal of the camp is to give adolescents the opportunity to take on responsibilities," says the camp director.

Many "ranch camps" in the Southwest offer boys and girls a vacation on horseback. The ranch staff consists of Western cowboys and cowgirls. Each camper is assigned a horse for the season. He rides his mount on pack trips, competes in games on horseback, and learns to feed, saddle, and curry the horse.

There are camps for the handicapped, camps for budding musicians, camps for heavyweights who want to slim down, science camps, and there are even traveling camps.

"Specialties are fine," says Jack Franks, director of Rawhide Ranch, in Woodstock Township, New York, "but every camp has the same goal—to return each child home a healthier, happier, and wiser person. That's what this business is all about."

6

CHAIN SUPERMARKET

THE SUPERMARKET of the 1970's sells more than 7,500 different items. It is likely to employ over one hundred people. Its cash registers may take in over $2,000,000 a year. Such an enterprise is aptly named; it is definitely a *super*market.

The idea of a market, a place where buyers and sellers meet, was known to civilizations of the past. As long ago as 1200 B.C., Chinese merchants traded goods by means of organized markets. In ancient Athens, jewelry, clothing, cutlery, and perfumes were sold in markets that were organized by public officials. These included a labor market, where workingmen, both slave and free, assembled to meet prospective employers.

The term "market" comes from early Rome. *Mercari* was the Latin term meaning "to buy." The meeting of buyers and sellers was called a *mercatus*. Our word "market" was derived from this term.

Market economy reached a high state of development during Roman times. In the city of Rome itself, per-

A German market of the sixteenth century

manent shops and public buildings were constructed around the principal market, which was known as the Forum. Separate markets were established for the sale of meat, fish, and vegetables.

The markets of Rome were created and regulated by the state, a custom that was revived during feudal times. Landowners of the day required mer-

"""

chants to pay a fee for the use of market stalls and a tax on the goods they sold as well.

Market customs and rules were spread throughout the world by merchants who traveled from country to country. In Europe, in England particularly, the market system reached its peak during the fifteenth century, but then came decades of decline. The rise of guilds and trade unions, which had the power to control the supply of certain goods and so control the price, reduced the influence of the market, where free competition was the order of the day.

Still, when the first English colonists came to the New World, they brought the market idea with them. In Boston, in 1633, the Court of Assistants passed an order creating an open market every Thursday. As the city's commercial life became busier, the order was amended to allow the market to be held three times a week, on Tuesday, Thursday, and Saturday. In 1676, Sir Edmund Andros, governor of New York, declared before the New York City Council that a "fitt house" was being built to house New York City's market.

Each of these early markets was

Each item on the supermarket shelf gets a carefully allotted amount of space. "Stockouts," out-of-stock items, cost sales and lose customers

64

spread over a large open area and consisted of many stalls, booths, or departments which were leased to individual proprietors. Markets of this type foreshadowed the day of the supermarket.

As early as 1900, the firm of Henke and Pillot operated a supermarket-type store in Houston, Texas, but the first widespread development of supermarkets took place on the West Coast about 1925, with a concentration of stores in the Los Angeles area. Los Angeles, unlike major cities of the East, had no efficient means of public transportation, no subways, elevated trains, or trolley cars. The residents of Los Angeles were automobile-minded, however. In 1928, 35 percent of the residents of Los Angeles owned their own cars, a figure much higher than the national average for the day.

Another fact is important. Parking facilities in the downtown area of the city were severely limited. These circumstances combined to trigger the development of outlying areas, where land was relatively plentiful and reasonably priced.

Huge open-front stores, called "drive-in markets," began to make their appearance. Each of these con-

Nonfood items, like sewing supplies and equipment . . .
and books and magazines are now supermarket staples

65

sisted of a group of food stores in a one-story building, with ample parking facilities. One of these, the Chapman Park Drive-In Market of Los Angeles, had parking facilities for 495 cars and was considered a wonder of its day.

Supermarkets in the East got their start during the Great Depression of the early 1930's. Business activity was at a low ebb. Unemployment was widespread, and many of those who were employed saw their wages sharply cut. Against this background, Michael Cullen opened the first of the "cheapy" markets. These stores emphasized what people of this period wanted most—cut-rate prices. By the end of 1932, King Kullen Markets, as Cullen named his stores, were operating in eight locations, and other cheapy chain operators were entering the field. These included the Big Bear Markets, The Price Wrecker, and The Price Crusher.

Cheapies were set up in abandoned warehouses or empty department stores or factories. Their interiors were primitive by today's standards. Lights glared from unsightly fixtures. Ceilings were unpainted and concrete floors untiled. Merchandise was piled on shelves and tables in helter-skelter fashion. Yet people flocked to the cheapies. One study discloses that some customers drove as far as fifty miles to shop.

The drive-in market of Los Angeles and the East Coast cheapies demonstrated that the supermarket operation was economically sound. During the late 1930's, when the country began to emerge from the period of the Great Depression, many brand-new supermarkets were built. They stressed low prices, but attractive appearance as well.

During this period chain operators began to enter the supermarket field. The Great Atlantic & Pacific Tea Company, Kroger, First National Stores, and American Stores, chains which had always operated small economy stores, began opening experimental supermarkets. The profit records of these stores convinced the chains that the supermarket was the store of the future.

The swing to supermarkets was dramatic. In 1929, A & P operated 15,150 small economy stores and not a single supermarket. By 1939, the number of small economy stores had been reduced to 7,902 and the company had 1,119 supermarkets in operation. In 1970, there were approximately 4,700 A & P supermarkets in operation. The small economy store had gone the way of the buggy whip.

The expansion of the supermarket industry slowed to a halt during the years of World War II, 1941 through 1945. There were shortages of some food items and others were rationed by the Federal Government. Gasoline was rationed, too, and the family automobile spent much more time in the garage. In addition, building materials were not available to construct new stores.

But during the postwar period, the supermarket industry went through

66

another period of rapid growth. The nation's population began to shift from the cities to the suburbs, opening up thousands of new locations for stores. Stores got bigger to make room for the hundreds of nonfood items supermarkets began to feature, things like health and beauty aids, housewares, toys, stationery, and soft goods, that is, clothing and other textile products.

Stores became more splendid too. Customers were cooled by air conditioning and soothed by recorded music. Shopping for food became a form of entertainment for many a suburban housewife.

There are approximately 32,000 chain supermarkets in operation in the United States today. (The Federal Government defines a chain as any retailing organization with eleven or more outlets.) All these stores offer a dazzling array of food and nonfood items. They are self-service in nature and operate on a cash basis. And supermarkets have one other quality —low margin of profit. For every $100 in sales, the store averages slightly less than one dollar in profits. Very few other American industries operate on so slim a profit margin.

No two chain operators manage their stores in exactly the same manner. With some, stores are controlled directly from the chain's home office. Other stores are controlled by a traveling supervisor. And in still other cases, stores are divided into districts or regions and controlled by a regional management official. But no matter what method a chain uses, it gives a large amount of responsibility to the individual store manager. He is the key. He plans and supervises all store operations and sales programs, and while he may assign duties to those who work for him, the manager remains responsible to the chain headquarters for the efficiency of the store's operations.

Supermarket managers are developed in one of two ways. Often they are chosen for their in-store experience. Sometimes a high school boy takes a part-time job as a supermarket stock clerk or "bundler," packing customers' orders into bags or boxes. After he graduates from high school, he becomes a full-time employee, and gradually works his way up the ladder. He may become an assistant in the grocery or meat department and eventually a department supervisor.

Other young men follow a different route. They become store managers following college graduation, perhaps with a business degree.

But in either case, the man goes through a period of intensive training before he is assigned a store of his own. The training can involve as much as a full year of classroom instruction in the art of management, in directing and controlling a supermarket operation. Classes are conducted by specialists from university faculties and by management experts from different retail fields.

The period of classroom study is

followed by months of in-store training, with the manager-candidate working as an assistant in the various departments of the store. Even after he becomes a store manager, his training continues. Periodically he attends company seminars for advanced study and to meet and exchange information with other store managers.

Intensive training is important and so is experience. But the supermarket is such a vast enterprise, involving so many different activities, that the only way the manager of a store can hope to be successful is by organizing his work, delegating duties to those who work for him, and skillfully supervising them. In other words, the store manager must be a leader. Unless he has the quality of leadership, the store operation can become chaos.

A store manager can never act like a "big shot." He has to treat his employees with dignity. He has to be fair. He must never show any favoritism in scheduling vacations or days off.

He has to be a decisive person, one who answers questions frankly and has the ability to settle controversies. In other words, he has to know how to handle problems.

Employees feel secure working for a store manager with a thorough knowledge of his job. They realize that they can learn from such a person and with learning comes advancement.

A store manager has to exercise real control in order to win his employees' confidence and respect. When an employee blunders or fails to obey company rules, the manager must set the man straight. The other employees expect him to; they resent the manager who speaks about an employee's shortcomings to everyone but the employee himself.

Employees respond to the manager who is cheerful and enthusiastic. A pessimistic boss is likely to have sour-faced employees.

While the supermarket manager has authority over all store employees, he works directly with only a handful of them, principally with his department supervisors. Almost all supermarket operations involve four different departments: a grocery department, a meat department, a produce department, and a cash control department.

The manager of the grocery department is responsible for ordering all grocery items from the company's warehouse, and seeing to it that they are properly received, priced, and stocked. He also has these responsibilities for frozen food products, bakery goods, and most of the store's nonfood items.

Ordering is no simple task. The grocery manager has to order enough of each item so that his supply will not get too low before the next delivery. When a store runs out of an item, it is a serious matter. It loses sales; worse, it loses customers.

At one time, store managers were not concerned by out-of-stock items. It was generally believed that a customer would simply choose a substi-

68

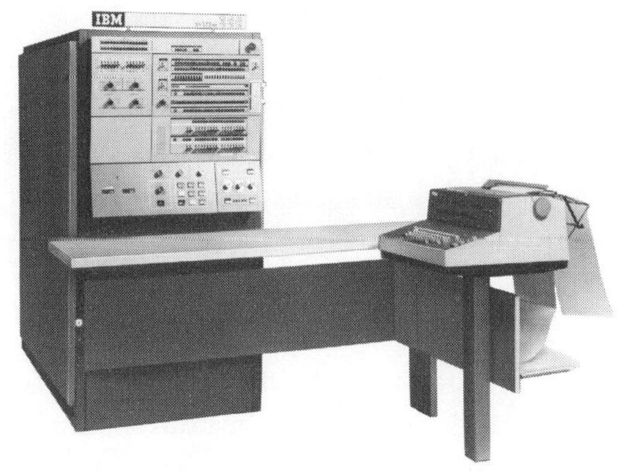

Large supermarket chains receive electronically transmitted supply orders from their stores on computer devices like this one

tute when her favorite item was not available. But recent studies show this to be untrue. In the case of toothpaste, instant coffee, floor wax, detergent, and many other items, the customer is not likely to switch brands.

The frozen food department is where "stockouts," out-of-stock items, occur most frequently. This is because the number of frozen food items is constantly increasing, but the storage and display space for these foods is limited.

The grocery manager also has to be careful not to overorder. Each store has only a limited amount of storage area. If the manager orders too much of any one item, he is likely to use up the storage space he needs for something else.

For speed and efficiency, modern supermarkets use a computer when ordering. Each store of a chain has an electronic transmitter at its command. To place an order, the store manager feeds a computer-prepared list of inventory items into the transmitter. He also feeds into it a roll of punched tape that contains the wanted quantity of each item.

The items the store requires are taken from the headquarters warehouse and loaded on a huge trailer truck. Before the truck leaves the warehouse, each truck door is sealed with a small metal band that bears a coded number. When the truck arrives at the store, one of the first things the manager does is check the seals to assure that they have not been broken or tampered with.

The day of delivery and the time of day are worked out carefully in advance, so that there will be store personnel available to check the load when it arrives. Every item ordered must be accounted for. If the store manager has ordered six cases of a particular brand of cornflakes, then he makes certain that he receives six cases.

Not every item a store requires comes from the company warehouse. Some grocery products and frozen foods are ordered direct from the manufacturer. These items must go through the same careful checking procedure when they are received.

After the order is received, each item has to be price-marked. Many grocery products are marked by a device called a "pogo stick," a wooden rod about ten inches long with a rubber stamp affixed to one end. The clerk inks the stamp, then imprints the package. There is a different pogo stick for each price.

Prices are imprinted before packages are removed from the case. To avoid missing a package or double marking one, the clerk is trained to move his hand in a precise pattern, beginning in the lower left-hand corner of the case and moving up one row, then down the adjacent row.

The marked items are then placed on the shelves, a chore often performed by a night crew of workers. A carefully measured amount of space is allotted to each item. How much space an item is assigned depends upon its turnover, the quantity sold in a given amount of time, usually one week. A fast-moving item gets more shelf space than a slow-moving item, provided they are of similar size.

But the amount of shelf space allotted any item is subject to change. For example, the entire sections devoted to soft drinks and fruit juices have to be expanded during the summer when sales of these products increase.

Once the items are on the shelf, they are checked frequently. Products like baby foods, cheese spreads, flour, peanut butter, cookies, and crackers bear code numbers. By reading the code, a clerk can tell when an item should be removed from the shelf. In this way the store management assures that its products are always fresh.

A package of cookies might carry this code: 06 30. The "06" refers to the month—June, the sixth month of the year. The "30" is the day of the month. This code number advises that the cookies must be taken off sale on June 30.

The manager of a supermarket's meat department is faced with a different set of responsibilities. In the average supermarket, the meat department accounts for 20 to 30 percent of the volume of business. But the department is even more important than these figures suggest.

"Meat makes the meal" is a well-known expression in the food industry. It means that the housewife plans the meal around the type of meat she selects. If she buys a porterhouse steak, she is also likely to buy mushrooms, baking potatoes, sour cream, green peas, salad fixings, and other items to serve with the steak. And she is almost certain to buy these items in the store where she makes her meat purchase.

For this reason, processing and merchandising keynote the operation of the meat department. Processing refers to cutting and trimming the meat in keeping with the housewife's wishes. Merchandising refers to packaging and displaying the meat in an attractive manner. Each meat package must be able to sell itself.

Many supermarket chains now wrap most cuts of meat in transparent plastic film. It enables the meat to be wrapped quickly and securely. More important, it adds to the meat's appeal. The label on each package must be easy to read. It must identify the item, give its weight, the price per pound, and the total price.

It takes a vast store of knowledge to qualify as a meat department manager. Pork, lamb, beef, veal, poultry, and fish each involve different cutting methods and merchandising techniques, and the meat manager must know them all.

The manager of the produce department has to be an expert in the care and handling of fruit and vegetable products. Supermarkets stock and sell slightly more than one hundred different produce items. Some have to be kept iced and wet, like cabbage, lettuce, and spinach. Others must be kept cold but merely moist, like peas and broccoli. Still others have to be kept iced and moist, but their tops have to be kept dry. Beets, radishes, and turnips are in this category.

Then there are scores of fruits and vegetables that can never be iced and must be kept dry. Apples, bananas, corn, cucumbers, squash, and tomatoes are examples of these.

The handling and storage of fruits and vegetables is only one aspect of the produce manager's job. He also has to know where and when to buy the various items of produce, and how much to pay. He has to know how to package and display each item.

Take the case of strawberries, one of the most profitable of all berries, and, during certain times of the year, one of the best of all income producers.

The manager of the produce department must be skilled in creating attractive displays

The produce manager must be aware that California, Oregon, Louisiana, and Washington are the major strawberry-growing states. California, which produces 25 percent of the nation's crop, offers strawberries throughout the year. A produce manager who represents a supermarket in the northeastern United States might buy his strawberries from Florida and Louisiana early in the year. He would deal with local farmers in the spring and early summer.

He would know that strawberries are among the most perishable of fruits and treat them accordingly. When receiving a shipment, he would have the berries inspected for mold or decay. He would always sell the ripest berries first. At the peak of the season, he would be likely to display related products with the strawberries, like whipped cream, shortcakes, and dry cereals.

Besides the grocery, meat, and produce departments, the manager of a supermarket supervises one other department—cash control. The manager of this department is responsible for the checkout operation, where the customer's purchases are itemized and her money collected. He supervises the cashiers and bundlers, training them and setting their work schedules.

Managers strive constantly to achieve a smooth flow of customers through the check-out counters. In many stores, policy dictates that no more than three customers are to be made to line up at any one register. When a line of more than three customers forms, the next register is opened.

An alert store manager keeps an eye on the carriage storage area to get an indication of what customer traffic is going to be. If there are few carts in the storage area, he knows that a period of heavy traffic is soon to follow.

Store managers drill their checkers to follow a carefully rehearsed routine in every phase of each transaction. The moment immediately after the order has been totaled, and just before the money has been collected is crucial. As the customer hands over the money, the checker is trained to repeat the

Check-out clerks must be both fast and efficient

total amount of the order, and then, using the words "out of," announce the denomination of the bill he has received. For example, a checker might say, "$9.27 *out of* ten dollars."

The bill the checker accepts is placed *across* the bill slots in the register drawer. If there is any disagreement as to the amount the checker has received, the bill is right there as evidence.

Each checker is instructed to count out the change to himself, counting upward from the amount of the order to the amount received. Some cash registers are equipped with automatic change computers. In such cases, the clerk counts out the amount of change due to the customer beginning with the largest bill and working down to the smallest coin.

After the checker has taken the change from the drawer, he tears off the customer's tape and next counts out her

72

Check-cashing is a service many super-markets offer

STOP & SHOP, INC.

change. "Thank you," he says, and turns to the register to put the bill in its appropriate slot and shuts the drawer.

Besides operating the register and handling cash, checkers are responsible for keeping the check-out area clean. Courtesy on the part of checkers is a must. "We want our checkers to convey a sincere 'come back again soon' feeling," says one store manager.

Most supermarkets evaluate the performance of each checker every few weeks. The store manager, or his cash department supervisor, picks out a sample order containing a wide variety of food items. A person not known to the checker takes the order through each check-out counter. Each checker is graded on the basis of courtesy, accuracy, and overall efficiency. The procedure is repeated each month.

All supermarkets cash checks as a service to their customers. But a "bad check," one not collectable and therefore worthless, can represent a serious loss. Check-cashing is one of the most strictly controlled phases of the supermarket operation. The manager of the cash control department examines each check carefully. The amount must be within a certain limit, and the customer, if not known to the manager, must show proper identification.

Some chain stores issue identification cards to their regular customers to be used when cashing checks. Other stores use a camera that takes a simultaneous photo of the customer, the check he wishes to cash, and his identification. The use of such systems works to reduce the number of bad checks presented for payment.

Bad checks represent only one type of loss supermarkets are subject to. Shoplifting represents another and even more serious one.

Unfortunately for the nation's supermarkets, shoplifting is a simple crime to commit. What is even worse, many shoplifters do not even consider the act to be a crime. Store managers have different methods for dealing with suspected pilferers.

73

"If I spot a customer slipping something into her purse, I let her," says the manager of a supermarket in Detroit. "Then I assign two clerks to follow her around the store. When she realizes she is being watched, she usually puts the item back and then leaves the store."

Other store managers prefer to confront the suspected pilferer. "I introduce myself to the suspect," says the manager of a Skokie, Illinois, store. "Then I say something like, 'Is this the first time you've ever done something like this?' The idea, of course, is to get her to admit her guilt."

Some stores hire uniformed guards in an effort to reduce stealing. Curved circular mirrors mounted near ceiling level are also used to help detect shoplifters at work.

Other stores rely on closed circuit television, with the cameras directed toward shelves shoplifters favor. One camera is usually mounted above the entrance door and the picture it transmits is shown on a receiving set that greets customers when they enter the store. "People see themselves on the screen when they walk in," a store manager explains, "and right away they know we're serious about shoplifting."

Security experts say that shoplifting is most serious in big-city stores. In small communities, where the residents are likely to know the manager personally, shoppers are more honest.

Shoplifting is not the only form of pilferage. Occasionally a housewife will switch price labels from one item

Pilfering is a constant problem for supermarket managers

to another to get a bargain. "This is a constant problem," says a New Jersey store manager. A woman will remove a label from a package of chopped sirloin and put it on a rib roast of beef or some other expensive cut of meat.

"The only way you can guard against this is to train your cashiers to be careful about all meat purchases. A rib roast that costs $1.09 doesn't make sense."

Sometimes it is the employees who are the pilferers. "I have to admit that my store loses most of its money at the check-out counter," says the manager of a Baltimore store. "A relative or close friend of the cashier comes up to the check-out counter with a big order. The cashier doesn't bother to charge the relative for some of the items and rings up an amount less than the marked price for others. Maybe the person ends up paying $10 for $25 worth of merchandise. That kind of thing kills us.

"You have to be watchful to pre-

74

vent this from happening. After a while you get so you can look at a shopping cart and estimate with a good degree of accuracy the value of the goods it contains. So if you see what looks to be a $25 order going through for $10, you do something about it."

The loss of shopping carts also cuts into store profits. The word "loss" is a polite term. Actually, they are stolen. The disappearance of a shopping cart is not a small matter. Each cart costs anywhere from $30 to $50.

City residents use the carts to wheel their laundry to the laundromat. Apartment superintendents use them to carry their tools and maintenance supplies from floor to floor. To city youngsters, carts are playthings, like wagons or bicycles. In suburban areas, shopping carts are often damaged beyond repair in the supermarket's parking lot.

Some stores report losing as many as fifty carts a month. Stores can't afford to hire the additional employees necessary to keep watch over carts, but some managers have reduced thefts by enclosing storefronts with steel fencing. The barrier exits are large enough to permit a customer to pass through but not a shopping cart.

"Getting good full-time help is another problem we have today," says Aime LaMontagne, manager of an East Hartford, Connecticut, supermarket for the Stop & Shop chain. "We don't have too much difficulty getting part-time employees. We get housewives who want to work as part-time checkers, and high school youngsters are willing to come in after school and stock shelves.

"Getting experienced managers for the grocery or meat departments is not a problem either. People are constantly being prepared for these positions through company training programs.

"But try to get a full-time stock clerk. Maybe the job has a poor image. Maybe it doesn't pay enough. Whatever the reason, it's hard finding full-time stock clerks today. And they're very much needed."

Store managers are constantly conducting promotions to increase sales. Sometimes the promotion effort concerns only one department, and at other times it involves the store as a whole, but all promotions are planned with the basic idea of attracting more customers, generating increased sales, and building goodwill.

These promotions almost always involve bargain prices. Three times a year, a large West Coast chain will sell items like canned tomatoes in five- or six-can units at a cost of a dollar per unit. The customer is allowed to buy one more can for just one cent. "Look What Your Pennies Buy at Mayfair's Giant One Cent Sale," the firm's newspaper advertisements declare. Canned vegetables, canned fruits, frozen orange juice, and frozen vegetables are other items offered during the sale.

A Mobile, Alabama, supermarket boosts sales with a "giant" promotion. All the large- and "family"-sized packages in the store are specially priced. To attract attention to the sale, large

Tie-in displays are popular. Here fruit syrups are paired with ice cream

paper footprints are pasted on the floor, leading customers from the store entrance to the specially priced items. Store employees wear footprints pinned to their pockets. Window signs, store banners, and newspaper advertisements hail the "Giant-Size Savings."

Children have a striking influence on supermarket sales. With this in mind, a Midwest chain of supermarkets has developed a promotion aimed square at the youngsters. Called "Kids Week," it is held during June, right at the beginning of summer vacation.

Each store involved in the promotion celebrates the joys of no more school. Suppliers of cookies, ice cream, and soft drinks give out samples of their products in the stores. One store holds a dog show with prizes going to the smallest dog, the biggest, the dog with the longest tail, the biggest ears, etc. Another store holds a watermelon-eating contest. A third store rents an airplane to fly over its parking lot and drop five hundred small plastic balls, each containing a certificate good for a small prize.

Special newspaper advertisements and in-store display material promote the "Kids Week" theme. The foods that children like the best are the ones that are bargain-priced: in the bakery department, cookies and doughnuts; in the meat department, chopped beef and hot dogs; and in the produce department, watermelon and bananas.

In-store displays are another method the store owner uses to increase sales. Sometimes the products on display are dictated by the headquarters office. Other times the store manager decides. But in any case it is likely that the products are ones that sell fast and represent a high profit.

One of the most effective display areas in any store is the "island end," the "island" being the shelf area between aisles. Two different but related products usually make up each island-end display. The central portion of the display might feature a cake mix, while the "wings" might be given over to frosting mixes, or a tomato sauce and a particular brand of spaghetti might be the products.

Some supermarkets use trading stamps in an effort to increase sales. When a customer makes a purchase, she is given stamps as a premium. Certain quantities of stamps can be ex-

76

changed for various household articles or gift items.

But the use of trading stamps as promotion medium is on the decline. "We're getting away from the giveaway image," says the manager of a Cleveland supermarket. "These days we prefer to be known for our low prices." Industry experts predict that the use of trading stamps in supermarkets will continue to diminish.

What's ahead for the American supermarket? What will the new store of 1975 and beyond be like? For one thing, say the experts, stores of the future will be larger, much larger. *Progressive Grocer* magazine predicts that the "typical" new store of 1975 and beyond will be 30 percent larger than stores of the 1960's.

Larger stores are needed to display the ever-increasing number of new products. By 1975, the average store is expected to carry 10,000 different items. Many more nonfood and specialty items will be featured. There will be departments selling delicatessen foods, cut flowers and plants, gardening supplies, and prescription drugs. Tomorrow's supermarket is likely to have a luncheonette and a carry-out food section. Much more space will be given to fruit and vegetable displays. Frozen foods will have more variety and greater importance.

The store of the future will provide the housewife with a great deal more in the way of service and information. Some chains are planning Customer Service Centers, where hostesses will demonstrate new products, present menu ideas and recipes, and distribute information on the day's food and meat bargains.

Food has always been a cash business, but in some areas supermarkets are experimenting with credit cards and report favorable results. One day in the future the housewife might be able to say "Charge it!" in her local supermarket.

The term "supermarket" itself might

Stock control and inventory are basic to the supermarket operation

be scrapped. For a store that displays and sells 10,000 different items, boasts an array of departments offering non-food items, features a restaurant or a luncheonette, offers a hostess service to answer housewives' queries, and grants credit, too, might more appropriately be called a *super* supermarket.

7

GENERAL AVIATION AIRPORT

WHAT IS "GENERAL AVIATION"? The term refers to the whole range of more than 100,000 aircraft engaged in recreational, instructional, and business flying, the nation's non-airline, nonmilitary aircraft.

Who uses general aviation? Engineers use general aviation planes to inspect terrain, lumbermen to survey timber acreage, ranchers to round up stray cattle, real estate men to perform land surveys, and farmers to spray crops. Doctors, lawyers, manufacturers, distributors, retailers, and warehousers all use general aviation aircraft. Any person who is seeking to accomplish more things in less time is likely to join the list.

Airports to serve general aviation started as long ago as 1903, the year the Wright Brothers made their now historic flight over the white sands at Kitty Hawk, North Carolina. According to the Federal Aviation Administration, there are about 5,000 general aviation airports in operation today.

In its simplest form, the general aviation airport is simply a strip of level ground up to 2,000 feet in length and 300 feet in width. It may be turf or asphalt-surfaced. Ground facilities consist of a single, one-room building that serves as ready room for pilots and

A pilot checks weather conditions received via teletype before going aloft

offers a public telephone that can be used to call the U.S. Weather Bureau for weather information. It is likely that the only other ground support facility is a wind sock, a long, tapered cloth sleeve fixed to a pole and mounted on the building's roof to indicate wind velocity and direction.

A general aviation airport of this size is usually operated by only one man. He owns his own aircraft and is the operation's general manager, chief pilot, and head flying instructor.

At the other end of the scale is the large, prosperous, and technically sophisticated operation, which may be known as an "Executive Aircraft Terminal." As the regional headquarters for all types of general aviation aircraft, it offers a number of concrete runways, each at least a mile in length, and adjacent taxi strips and loading areas. It boasts hangars for aircraft, maintenance and repair shops, and a modern passenger terminal. There are elaborate air traffic control facilities and a direct communication link with the U.S. Weather Bureau. It may em-

This general aviation airport is located near Albany, Oregon.
It is owned and operated by the city

ploy well over a hundred people.

A general aviation airport can be owned and operated as a private venture by an individual or a corporation, but often it is operated by a city, county, or some other unit of the local government. In many cases, the community establishes an "authority" to run the airport.

The authority is empowered to purchase necessary goods and services from local business enterprises, and to hire its own employees. Often the authority engages the services of a full-time professional airport manager. It becomes his responsibility to direct the operation and maintenance of all airport facilities.

The manager's principal responsibilities are likely to concern the airport's various revenue sources, and chief among these is likely to be the renting of aircraft. Many general aviation airports provide a wide range of aircraft for charter or long-term lease, every type of plane from a small single-engine, single-seat craft, to a twin-engined jet. Some airports also offer helicopters for rent.

The airport's rental customers are likely to vary according to the region. Hereford Municipal Airport in Hereford, Texas, an agricultural community, provides aircraft for crop dusting and spraying, for fertilizing and seeding. Planes out of the Hereford field are used by farm equipment sales agencies and grain suppliers, and to ship out lettuce and carrots, chief products of the region.

Often the airport staff includes instructors for those who want to learn to fly

Hayward Air Terminal in Hayward, California, has altogether different types of customers. Hayward is an important distribution center for the heavily populated San Francisco Bay Area, and its airport is one of the busiest general aviation airports in the United States. There is a landing or takeoff every one and one half minutes. Aircraft rented to or belonging to hundreds of different business and industrial enterprises use the field.

The flight services such an airport offers are likely to include a flying school, which furnishes instructors and dual-equipped aircraft to those who wish to learn to fly. The general aviation airport also sells aircraft, both new and used.

Some airports charge fees to private aircraft for the use of landing areas. The Federal Aviation Administration has consistently opposed this policy, however. The FAA has felt that landing fees tend to curb airplane use, checking the growth of the aviation industry in general. In cases where landing fees are charged, the amount depends upon the size of the aircraft and the number of passengers or the weight of the cargo it carries.

Most general aviation airports have hangar space available on a rental basis

A second important source of general aviation airport income comes from the various "line" services the operation offers. These include the rental of hangars to aircraft owners, either metal, frame T-shaped hangars or large storage hangars, each of which can accommodate many aircraft. Airport operators also rent "tie-down" facilities. A tie-down is an open parking area with access to the airport taxiway, where the plane can be secured by rope to a fixture in the ground.

Line services also include aircraft maintenance and repair. A large airport is likely to hold a certificate from the Federal Aviation Administration as an "approved repair service" for aircraft of various types. The operation will be staffed and equipped to perform engine and airframe maintenance, to maintain and repair radio and electronic equipment. The sale of fuel, oil, and replacement parts also provides income.

There is an assortment of nonaviation services that can provide revenue too. A snack bar or a restaurant is one example. Invariably the operator of the airport will lease the food service operation to someone with know-how and experience in the field.

If he has a busy operation, the airport owner is not likely to have any difficulty attracting other concessionaires. A newsstand, a gift shop, automobile rental agencies—all of these can provide income, so long as the airport has floor space or buildings to accommodate such operations.

A good amount of the manager's time has to be devoted toward keeping the airport's many and varied facilities in first-class operating condition. Foremost among these are the systems used to direct and control aircraft.

At a large airport, air traffic is controlled by two-way radio that enables the airport tower to communicate with the pilots of planes about to take off or land. The air traffic control system may also provide for on-instrument approaches to the airport when weather conditions make visual approaches impossible.

Air traffic is sometimes controlled by locally established "rules of the road" and light signals. For example, a steady green light directed toward an ap-

*Among the "line" services that airports offer are fuel . . .
and "tie-down" facilities*

proaching aircraft means the field is clear for landing. The pilot rocks his plane's wings to acknowledge the signal.

At small general aviation airports a "segmented circle" is another standard air traffic control aid. It gives essential landing information to the pilot of an approaching aircraft. At least one hundred feet in diameter, the segmented circle is constructed by laying wood or metal panels on the ground. A wind sock is mounted atop a T-shaped landing direction indicator in the center of the circle.

The system also includes a number of L-shaped segments arranged outside the circle, one "L" for each runway. The foot of each "L" indicates the direction aircraft are to use when approaching the related runway.

If the airport is used at night, lighting is another essential navigational aid. The lighting system is likely to include runway edge lights, a rotation beacon, a lighted wind indicator, and exit lights for all taxiways.

But communications and navigation equipment represent only one aspect of the airport manager's responsibility as maintenance supervisor. He or one of his staff members must make periodic inspections of the airport's terminal buildings, traffic surfaces, and grounds. The idea, of course, is to spot potential problems and make repairs

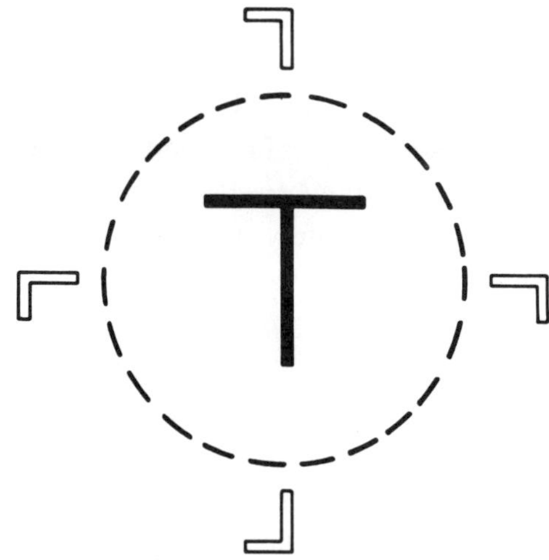

From the air a "segmented" circle may look like this

83

right away. This policy prevents small problems from becoming major sources of trouble.

Take the case of a concrete runway. The manager's inspection seeks to determine whether there are any open joints between concrete slabs, or any slab "pop-outs" or "blowups." He looks for random cracks in the runway surface, and checks to see how previously sealed cracks and joints are wearing.

He carefully inspects the concrete for scaling, chipping, or splintering. He looks for surface irregularities, like dish-shaped depressions that are known as "birdbaths," or surface ruts called "washboards."

As soon as a trouble spot is detected, it has to be repaired. In the case of random cracking, the cracks are hollowed out with a special router equipped with hardened steel tip. A newer method involves the use of a diamond-bladed saw. Once the crack is opened, it is cleaned, then sealed.

Repairing erosion damage to runways and broken surfaces and filling in potholes are only one aspect of the comprehensive safety program the airport manager must adopt. Hazards can also be created by snow, ice, or slush. There have been instances of aircraft swerving off runways because of slippery conditions or colliding with snowbanks adjacent to runways or taxiways. Every airport manager must have an efficient, thoughtfully planned snow removal program.

The field drainage system has to be checked frequently. Grass, bits of pa-per, small sticks, and other debris can clog catch basins. Should this happen, a runway might become flooded during a storm.

If the approach zone to the airport is a wooded area, it has to be checked once or twice a year for new tree growth. Some trees may have to be trimmed or removed.

Birds are still another problem. As an aircraft is taking off or landing, a bird can strike the propeller causing serious damage, or an aircraft encountering a flock of birds may have its windshield shattered. A small aircraft once collided with a loon near Bakersfield, California. The plane's tail section was destroyed and a crash resulted which was fatal to both the pilot and his passenger.

Engineers of the Federal Aviation Administration have found that bird strikes usually occur at altitudes of 2,500 feet or less. Approximately twenty-five different species of birds have been involved in the strikes, with gulls and starlings more frequently than any others.

Some airport managers seek to scare away roosting birds by using scare devices, such as carbide exploders or recordings of bird distress calls. "This does not get to the basic problem," says the FAA. "The solution is to make the airport unattractive to birdlife."

This can be accomplished by filling in swamps and ponds near the airport, clearing away berry- and seed-bearing shrubs and trees, and covering edible waste dumps and, in general, denying birds nearby food, water, and roosting areas.

Keeping financial records is important to every type of business, and the air base operation, small or large, is no exception. Carefully kept records give the operator an idea of how much working capital he has on hand, what his expenses are and which ones might be excessive, and how much profit his business is showing.

He employs bookkeepers or an accounting service to itemize all expenses relating to his business, including the sums he pays out in wages. The employee payroll, incidentally, is likely to be his biggest single expense item.

He keeps sales records that list every item he sells, such as fuel and aircraft parts. He also keeps an inventory record of parts and accessory items to help him in planning future purchases. His sales records include a daily accounting of sums he receives for hangar rental and flight instruction.

He also maintains a record of money

This is an island airport located near Knoxville, Tenn. Note the segmented circle in the left foreground

owed to him and money he owes to his suppliers. These are known as accounts receivable and accounts payable records. From all these records he draws up a monthly profit and loss statement, and, perhaps every six months, a balance sheet. This gives him a clear idea of his financial position and the worth of the business.

The Federal Aviation Administration has recognized a serious problem concerning the nation's general aviation airports. By 1979, the FAA estimates, there will be 203,000 general aircraft, more than twice the number in operation in 1966.

To provide for these aircraft, at least 700 new airports will be needed, says the FAA. And about one half the nation's 5,000 existing general aircraft airports will have to be substantially improved.

The problem is even more grave than these statistics predict. Community opposition to airports is beginning to develop in many areas. The public does not object to airports in themselves but to the aircraft noise and surface traffic congestion often associated with them. These were not serious problems until the coming of the jet age. The screaming whine of the jet engine attacks the eardrums with a far greater ferocity than the throaty roar of a piston-engined plane. And with the jets has come a sharp upswing in the use of the airplane by the public, creating heavy surface traffic congestion.

In addition, today more people live closer to airports then ever before. Many of our airports were laid out years ago in completely rural areas, when the takeoff of a plane disturbed only grazing farm animals. But in recent decades the suburbs have pushed farther and farther from the central city. Those airport managers who have not sold out to real estate interests now often find themselves surrounded— literally—by hostile homeowners.

Chester Bowers, Director of Airports Service for the FAA, stated in 1969, "In its most dire aspect, social opposition may ultimately force the closure of many close-in airports." Indeed, community opposition to the very existence of his airport may be the most serious problem to face the airport manager.

TELEVISION STATION

WHAT TYPE OF PERSON runs a television station? A report by Charles Winick, a noted specialist in the study of occupational roles, disclosed that the general manager of a television station is likely to be a relatively young person and a hard worker. He was born in a small town. He saw military service overseas. He enjoys challenge and is unbothered by pressure.

His duties and responsibilities vary according to the size of the station he manages, but in almost every case he supervises three key departments—programming, sales, and engineering. His job and what he does is also affected by the type of station he manages, that is, whether it is affiliated with one of the three television networks—NBC (the National Broadcasting Company), ABC (the American Broadcasting Company), or CBS (the Columbia Broadcasting System). If it is not affiliated with a network, the station is known as an "independent."

A network is simply a group of stations that receives its programming from a common source. Ninety-five percent of the nation's slightly more than 800 television stations are network-affiliated.

If a local station belongs to the ABC Television Network, it means the station receives fourteen to eighteen hours of programming from ABC every day. It also means that the station receives a good portion of its income from ABC for carrying network-originated commercial announcements.

Obviously, operating a network-affiliated station makes for a much different set of problems from running an independent station. Since the independent does not receive programming from the network, the station manager has to fill out the programming schedule on his own by creating "live" programs or buying and presenting film.

Most large cities have at least one independent station. There are three independents in New York and four in Los Angeles.

Stations also differ as to their technical character. Some television stations are known as VHF stations and others, a smaller number, are UHF. These designations refer to the two different types of carrier waves that are used to transmit television signals from the station to the receiver. VHF is an abbreviation for *very high frequency*; UHF means *ultra high frequency*.

The band of frequencies over which the carrier waves are sent is called a channel. The Federal Government has established channels 2–13 for VHF broadcasting and channels 14–83 for UHF.

Generally, the VHF stations are larger, more influential, and show a greater profit than their UHF cousins. The reasons for this are largely historical.

In television's days of commercial infancy during the late 1940's, the Federal Government allocated only VHF channels, no UHF. Naturally, the television sets manufactured during those years, and through a good part of the decade of the 1950's as well, were made to receive only the VHF signal.

It soon developed that the few VHF channels were inadequate to provide a truly nationwide television system, so in 1952 the FCC opened up the UHF wavelengths for commercial broadcasting. But few people could tune in UHF channels because their sets were equipped to receive only VHF programming. In addition, many of the new UHF channels were beset with technical difficulties that interfered with the quality of the picture they transmitted.

The Federal Government acted to improve the situation. In 1956, the maximum power of UHF stations was increased, and this overcame most of the programming problems. In 1962, Congress passed a law requiring manufacturers to equip all television sets manufactured after April, 1964, with both VHF and UHF channels.

Many UHF stations are devoted to educational broadcasting. These are often referred to as ETV (educational television) stations. Most educational television stations are owned and operated by school systems, colleges, or universities. Their purpose is to furnish education programs to teachers and students, but they also provide the public at large with programming of an educational nature.

Educational broadcasting received a substantial boost early in 1952 when the Federal Government made channel assignments to 242 communities for noncommercial, educational broadcasting. As a result, nearly every city and town in the United States now has its own ETV station.

Whether a station is network-affiliated or independent, VHF or UHF, it features one standout characteristic: it never shuts down. Programming goes on unceasingly, 17 or 18 hours a day, on the average, and a few stations operate almost around the clock. There is never a holiday; every station operates 365 days a year.

There is no seasonal reduction in programming hours either. A magazine will reduce the number of its editorial pages during the summer when advertisers cut back on expenditures, and the same is true of most newspapers. But television stations present the same amount of programming in the summer as in winter.

This characteristic puts a heavy responsibility on the station's program director. He is the person responsible for determining what programs are to be seen and when, although the final decision in such matters rests with the station's general manager.

In developing his station's schedule, the program director gets programs from three different sources. Programs supplied by the network fill out a major portion of the schedule. The other two sources are film and "live" productions, programs that are televised at the moment they are being presented.

One type of film available is the half-hour series show that has been shown previously on the network. Stations purchase the right to telecast these programs, called "reruns," from syndication companies. How much a station must pay for a syndicated film series often depends upon the size of the station and the competition for the series within the market. In Los Angeles, for example, there are seven television stations, and each of them may want to buy a newly available film series. There is spirited bidding and the price may skyrocket. But in smaller markets with fewer stations, film prices are lower.

Besides syndicated film, the station can also purchase feature films, which are full-length Hollywood motion pictures originally made for exhibition in

News, sports, and weather comprise the basic "live" programming for virtually all television stations

a theater. Many such films present well-known personalities and are expensively produced. Scores of such films have proved extremely popular with television audiences.

A good-sized station in a major market will purchase the rights to show a feature film four or five times. With careful planning, the program manager can win a good audience for the film each time it is shown. He schedules the showings six to eight months apart, and plans each on a different day of the week and at a different time period.

In a smaller market, where the potential audience is less, the station manager realizes that a feature film might earn adequate ratings for only one reshowing. He first presents the film as part of the station's nighttime schedule, and as much as a year later, he presents it during the day.

News, weather, and sports—these are the three types of programs produced live by virtually every commercial television station in the country. But the quality of such programs varies widely.

For example, the news program of one local station might simply show an announcer reading news reports from sheets of paper, and cut away occasionally to present a still photograph or a slide. If there is film, it is not likely to have sound accompanying it. The news, weather, and sports segments of the program are probably handled by the same announcer.

But another station might use its locally produced programs to establish a community-minded character for the station and to win high ratings as well. It might telecast an abundance of film of spot news events, and interviews with community officials and local business leaders. Local surveys or listener polls might be used to give additional interest.

Some stations produce a good deal more than merely the basic news-weather-sports type of program. WWJ-TV in Detroit is one example. Its local productions include a weekly zoo visit, an exercise show for women, an instruction program in woodworking, helpful hints on suburban living, and the telecast of actual religious services.

It takes considerably more personnel and equipment to present a live program than a film feature. Costs spiral upward as a result. This serves to limit the amount of live programming that stations can afford to present.

To the program director, the ideal viewer is the one who, upon awaking in the morning, immediately snaps on the television set to his station, and stays with the station throughout the broadcast day. Of course, the person who acts this way is incredibly rare. Television watchers tend to be selective. A viewer will watch a program until it concludes, and then is likely to check to see what is available on other channels. It is the job of the program director to try to limit this tendency and hold the viewer from the time the station begins telecasting right up until sign-off time.

Look at the listings of the television programs in your area. Notice how the schedule for each station follows a particular pattern, one that is likely to conform to the hour-by-hour interests of your family, and that changes as those interests change throughout the day.

During the morning broadcast hours, the television set often serves as an electronic baby-sitter. Children of school age have left. Mother is busy with the breakfast dishes, making beds, and other household chores. She is likely to turn on television to occupy her preschool youngsters. So the standard programming fare during the early morning hours includes cartoons, nursery-school-type programs like *Romper Room* or learning programs like *Sesame Street*.

By midmorning, mother is likely to have completed most of her household tasks and now begins to watch the set herself. The programs change in format, with cartoons giving way to situation comedies.

Sometimes a program director will attempt to win his share of the late-morning women's audience by scheduling an interview program or a panel show, programs that are devoted to subjects that interest housewives. But in doing so the program director realizes that he is running the risk of losing the child audience. The more usual practice is to follow the cartoons with comedy dramas, aiming for both the adults and the children. Program directors know that if the situation com-edies are filled with enough action, the preschoolers will watch.

At noontime the program lineup may change again. The schoolchildren are likely to be home for lunch. It is a busy period for most mothers. The television schedule again features cartoons, although some stations stay with situation comedies during this time, and a few have success with a news program.

In the early afternoon, there is a more determined effort to appeal to women than at any other time of the day. The program director realizes that the school-age children have returned to school, and that the pre-

Variety shows are usually slotted for late-afternoon audiences

schoolers are likely to be napping. Beginning at one o'clock the programming is likely to be made up of half-hour serialized dramatic programs.

The next important period of the day begins late in the afternoon, between four and five o'clock. The program director is now concerned about building an audience for those golden hours between seven thirty and eleven o'clock when viewership is at its peak.

The program director can seek to amass an audience by scheduling a feature film. A presentation of this type may be scheduled at five o'clock or five thirty to be followed by a news program.

Other stations prefer to program variety shows during the late-afternoon hours. Still other stations look to children to build their viewership, scheduling cartoons or half-hour film programs that have strong appeal for youngsters, presentations like *The Munsters* or *Batman*.

Network programs are featured from seven o'clock until ten or eleven o'clock. The family is together; ratings are at their peak.

For late-evening programming, most stations used to rely on feature films, but during the late 1960's this reservoir of programming material began to dry up. The films that were available had been rerun so many times that they no longer were capable of attracting large audiences. Besides, major Hollywood production companies were no longer making films in meaningful quantity. What happened was that many local stations began relying upon network "talk" shows for their late-evening programming. Popular personalities like Johnny Carson conduct the programs of this type.

When the late-evening talk show concludes, the station schedules a news report, often called the "late-late" news. By this time the audience has sharply dwindled, and so the program director produces the show as inexpensively as possible. Instead of a newscaster, a weatherman (or weather girl), and a sports reporter, the usual staff for an early-in-the-evening news presentation, the late-late news program is handled by only one announcer.

While stations throughout the country generally follow a program schedule such as just described, there are some differences from region to region. It is the responsibility of the program director to get to know his community and what happens inside its homes. He has to know what time the husbands leave for the day, when the wives are likely to be the busiest, whether the children are released from school at lunchtime, and so forth.

The program director has to know the social and personal habits of his community. For example, on the West Coast people do not watch late-night television to any great degree. But in the East, people stay up later. Naturally, this difference in viewing habits has a striking influence upon a station's program schedule.

If the program director does not keep in touch with the interests of his

92

community, he cannot do an intelligent job of programming. If a station in New York City were to present a telecast of a high school basketball game, it would attract very few viewers. But in Chillicothe, Ohio, high school basketball is a popular item.

Of course, the program director has to be aware of what the competition is doing when he prepares his schedule. A local station may concentrate on presenting programs for children, and almost all its daytime hours may be given over to cartoons and film programs that children enjoy. The station becomes known for this. The program director of another station in the same market might then be reluctant to schedule a cartoon show. "Why bother?" he figures. "All the kids are already watching Channel X." Instead of trying to win children as viewers, he sets out to win the women, and his schedule features adult dramas and game shows.

The best programs and the most skillfully developed program schedule are of little value unless the station is able to sell its programming time to advertisers. Every station has its sales department, men who call upon local advertisers to sell entire programs,

A New York City station presents mayoral candidates as part of its public service programming

WABC-TV, N.Y.

93

Advertisements like this one are meant to increase the size of a program's audience

minutes of commercial time, and portions of minutes.

The importance of the sales department cannot be underestimated. It is the income-producing arm of the station, and whether a station succeeds or fails depends upon the sales department. It is more than a coincidence that about 40 percent of all station managers have had training and experience in the sales field.

In selling their station's time, television salesmen lean heavily on demography, the science of vital and social statistics. Market research firms like the A. C. Nielsen Company and the American Research Bureau prepare frequent and detailed studies of the television audiences in every major market. A salesman uses the statistical information prepared by these firms to demonstrate the superiority of his station over other stations, or over competing forms of advertising, particularly newspapers.

The most important piece of information the salesman possesses concerns the size of the audience his station can deliver. The prospective advertiser wants to be assured that he is going to get maximum efficiency for the dollars he is going to spend, that his advertising message is going to reach the maximum number of people at the lowest possible cost.

The salesman can also report on the character of the audience. He can tell the prospective advertiser the number of men, women, and children who will be watching his commercial. And even more. He breaks the audience down into age groups. He tells the advertising manager what proportion of the audience is made up of women in the 18–34 age group, and what proportion are in the 18–49 group. He tells him how many teen-agers watch the program, and how many children ages 2–11, ages 6–11, etc.

Suppose the salesman calls upon a company that manufactures children's toys. "Look," he can say to the advertising manager, "here's a program that delivers an audience of 38,400 youngsters, ages 2–11. It's just right for your advertising message."

Once a salesman completes a sale, he immediately notifies his station's traffic department unit, which maintains a complete and up-to-the-minute list of scheduled commercial announcements. Each day the traffic unit prepares a detailed log for all departments that establishes the commercial placements on a minute-by-minute basis.

The people in the traffic unit never allow two competing products to be advertised in succession. There is at least a ten-minute separation between commercials by competing advertisers, and the separation is at least fifteen minutes at the better stations.

Television stations also derive a good part of their income from "spot announcements," those commercial messages seen within a non-network program or surrounding network presentations. "Spots" are also often programmed at the time when a station identifies itself.

Stations outside New York City hire spot sales companies to sell this time. There are about sixty such companies. In the television industry they are known as "TV reps" (representatives).

Every viewer sees the results of the work performed by a station's program department, and most of the business people of the community are familiar with what the sales department does, but the function of a station's engineering department is somewhat of a mystery. Yet the chief engineer has just as important a role in the station's operation as the program director or sales manager.

The chief engineer supervises the control room personnel whose job it is to monitor and regulate the quality of the picture that the station transmits. Engineers are also stationed at the station's transmitter, the part of the system that conveys the television program to the antenna, which, in turn, beams the program to home sets.

The engineering phase of the operation also includes the video tape department. Video tape itself is a three-inch wide plastic ribbon that employs a magnetic process to record electronic signals generated by television cameras and microphones. Once a program has been "taped"—recorded—it can be played back at any future time, in which case the electronic signals are converted back into picture and sound.

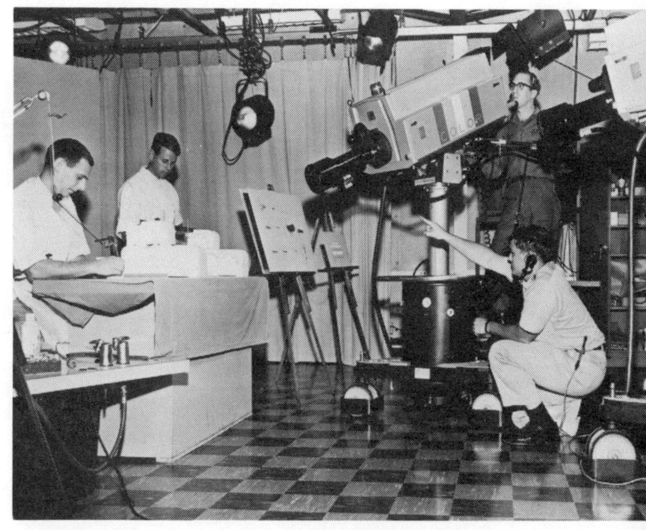

Engineers operate video tape equipment in a television studio . . . An engineer gives the go-ahead and the action begins

Not all engineers perform their duties in dimly lit control rooms. Suppose an important news event breaks. The station dispatches a team of men to cover it. One member of this team is an announcer and represents the program department, but all the others are engineers. These include a cameraman and a camera control director, an audio engineer, a lighting expert, and the crew's technical director. Other engineers staff the station's studio facilities when a live program is being telecast, and still others man film projection equipment in the case of film presentations.

The station's chief engineer has to keep alert to the industry's latest technical developments. Changes come rapidly in the world of television, and if the chief engineer does not take the time to become familiar with new types of equipment, his station can quickly fall behind the competition. In the late 1960's, there were still a sprinkling of stations without video tape equipment, and others that had not yet installed the necessary equipment to transmit color.

The chief engineer has to work closely with the station's two other major departments—programming and sales—to provide the technical knowhow required to carry out their programming wishes. Often the chief engineer can make valuable suggestions out of his fund of technical knowledge. He might, for instance, recommend to the program director how newscasts might be made more exciting through the use of swift video tape mobile units.

To keep informed about new equipment developments, the chief engineer reviews industry trade magazines, and attends conventions and trade shows where new equipment is displayed. The annual convention of the National Association of Broadcasters is a "must" on his schedule.

"We frequently recommend the purchase of new and improved tape projectors and film equipment," says Henry L. Dabrowski, chief engineer of WABC-TV, New York City. "We're constantly striving to transmit a picture of the highest quality with the best sound possible. If we feel some new

Station engineers must keep abreast of new equipment developments. Battery-powered video tape recorders are one recent innovation

equipment development will help us to better achieve this goal, then we don't hesitate to recommend it."

Besides programming, sales, and engineering, one other aspect of station operation is important. The nation's television stations do not own the airwaves. They belong to the public. The stations are granted permission to use the airwaves by the Federal Government, actually by the Federal Communications Commission.

Any individual or group wishing to own or operate a station must apply to the FCC for a license. The license is granted only if the Commission is assured that the station will operate "in the public interest, convenience, and necessity."

Besides licensing stations, the FCC also reviews the general programming of all stations to determine whether each is operating in the public interest. While the Commission does not dictate that certain percentages of broadcast time should be devoted to particular subjects, such as religious or educational topics, this matter is considered when the station applies for a renewal of its license. The nature, length, and number of the station's commercial announcements are also reviewed. An excess of commercials is not considered to be in the public interest.

9

COMMERCIAL PHOTOGRAPHY SERVICE

WHILE photography itself has a long history, beginning in the early 1700's, the camera did not come into widespread use until fairly recent times. The introduction of roll film by George Eastman in 1884 (which freed the photographer from the difficulty of coping with fragile and cumbersome equipment), the invention of the 35mm. camera in 1924, and the development of practical color film in 1934 were landmark events in the expansion of the photographic art.

As a result of these and other developments, pictures are now a basic means of communication. Pictures inform and document; they teach, entertain, and sell. All these needs are satisfied by the commercial photography service, sometimes called an "agency" or a "studio."

The special problems a photographer meets in managing and operating a business of his own are closely connected with where he chooses to locate. In small cities and towns, commercial photographers handle almost any type of assignment, from weddings and portraits to department store fashion shows and Little League baseball games.

But in large cities, photographers are much more specialized in the work they do. Some studios are known for fashion photography, others for their executive portraits. There are studios that specialize in photos to be used in publicity or advertising. There are legal photographic specialists, too, who provide lawyers with pictures of accident scenes or damage caused by fire or water, photos to be used as courtroom evidence.

Wedding photography is one basic source of income for a majority of the country's commercial studios. Wedding photography pays well, and the jobs are plentiful.

Studio owners consult the records of the local marriage license bureau and read the society pages to learn the names of young girls about to be married. Furniture stores and department stores, which number engaged couples among their better customers, can also provide leads, and sometimes

Many photographic services specialize; fashion photography is one well-known specialty

Other studios are known for portrait work

a photographer will learn of a prospective bride through a caterer or a clergyman.

In selling his service, it is standard practice for the photographer to meet with the girl several weeks before the event and show her an elegant album containing pictures of a previous wedding he has photographed. This portfolio, which contains both color and black-and-white photos, gives the girl a clear idea of what type of photos she can order. At the same time she and the photographer discuss prices.

In taking pictures of a wedding, the photographer strives to make the bride the star. The sequence of photos is likely to begin at the bride's home where last-minute adjustments are being made to her gown. The photographer snaps her picture as she leaves her home and at each different step of the occasion.

The groom is not considered nearly as important, and is photographed only as he may relate to the bride, as, for example, when he helps the bride cut the wedding cake. Photographers give the bride the more prominent role because the wedding is a once-in-a-lifetime occasion, her day of days. Also, by tradition it is the bride or her family who orders the photos and pays the bill.

Some photo studios offer "extras" to attract wedding business, providing prints and albums of various sizes and offering to supply the local newspaper with individual wedding portraits.

Photographers who run small studios

like to take pictures of children. A picture of a girl or a boy not only represents profit in itself, but, if it is attractive enough, can win the child's parents as customers. The mother or father may call upon the studio to have a portrait taken, or an older daughter may ask the studio to take pictures at her wedding. Indeed, taking pictures of children is one tried and proven method that many studios use to get established in a community.

Almost all children have their pictures taken in school each year. A local studio will make individual portraits of each student. The basic fee for such work is not large. The photographer earns most of his profits when the child's parents order framed portraits or wallet-size reprints.

The general area of school photography also includes high school yearbooks. Again, the studio earns the major part of its profit when the students order individual prints of their portraits to use as gifts for their friends, and for college and job applications. And parents usually want to order portrait-size prints.

Some studio owners specialize in baby pictures. Occasionally they work for hospitals, photographing newborn infants, but the more common practice is for the photographer to contact the parents soon after the birth. He is likely to suggest a series of photos over a one- or two-year period. By returning several times to photograph the child, the photographer increases the amount of the order.

Other photography services steer an entirely different course. Instead of weddings, children's photographs, and the like, they concentrate on building up a clientele of commercial and industrial accounts, and the advertising and publicity firms that represent companies of this type. Photographic agencies that do this type of work are usually found in the major cities.

Portrait photography is a special art

A large corporation requires many types of photographs: studio photos of its products to use in advertising and publicity and in sales bulletins and catalogs; photos of products being manufactured, and photos of the manufacturing plants themselves. The corporation requires portrait photographs of its executives. Any news event involving the company must be covered. In 1969, when the National Aeronautics and Space Administration sent the first men to the moon, on hand to record the blast-off were a great legion of photographers, representing the hundreds of companies involved in the construction of the rocket and its related equipment.

Minor news events have to be covered too. When a company breaks ground for a new building or launches a new product, a photographer is sure to be involved.

Most agencies employ full-time salesmen to solicit the business of large corporations. The salesman's starting point is often the Yellow Pages of the local telephone directory. He begins by calling on the biggest firms and works his way down the list. At his first meeting with a prospective client, the salesman is likely to show a portfolio of thirty or forty photographs that indicate the skill of the agency's photographers.

Once a commercial studio has been in operation for a time, it begins to accumulate photographs by the thousands. Most of these are photos that were taken on assignment for various clients, the resale rights having been retained by the studio owner. Others may be photos that the photographer has taken for his own enjoyment. But in either case, such photos can often be sold to a stock photo agency, providing another source of income.

A stock agency is one that maintains enormous files of photographs, classified by subject, for use by magazine editors, book publishers, daily newspapers, advertising agencies, and other clients. One such agency, Wide World Photos, Inc., offers more than 4,000,-000 pictures. An editor who requires a picture of some famous person, a landmark building, a winter scene, or a smiling baby—almost any subject at all—has only to call a stock agency and ask to see what is available.

A commercial studio with suitable photographs on file will enter into a working relationship with a stock agency. The studio receives a commission from the agency when one of its photos is sold to a client. The commission usually amounts to 50 percent of the selling price in the case of a black-and-white photo, and 60 percent for color.

Much of the studio manager's working day is likely to be devoted to the task of building business. He may be a gifted photographer and a skilled darkroom technician, but unless he also has talent as a salesman and public relations man, few people will ever know of his ability with a camera.

Often new business is gained through personal recommendation. "People are reluctant to give their money to strangers, no matter how fine their work may be," says Theodore Schwarz in his book *The Business Side of Photography*. True. What the photographer must do is make a "name" for himself in his community. He has to come to be recognized as a photographic authority.

There is a great deal he can do to achieve this recognition. He can organize amateur photography groups, perhaps serving as the moderator of a high school photography club. He can teach an adult education course in the subject.

He is very likely to become an active member of local civic and fraternal organizations, like the Rotary Club or the Kiwanis Club. Such organizations often require the services of a photographer to cover their social functions, make portraits of their officers, or provide documentation of their community service projects.

Celebrities can be important to a studio owner in helping him to become established. Suppose a well-known show business star is visiting his city. The photographer makes it a point to photograph the personality, and then displays the best of the pictures in his studio window. He does the same with well-known local political figures. People seeing these photos on display are impressed by them.

An alert photographer also uses the local news media to become better known. He appears on local radio and television interview programs to discuss such subjects as "Ten Do's and Don'ts When Having Your Picture Taken" or "The City's Ten Most Photogenic People." A Memphis, Tennessee, photographer writes a weekly column for a local newspaper containing helpful hints for amateur photographers. A Seattle studio owner conducts a photography question-and-answer column.

Many photographers keep on the lookout constantly for pictures that have news value—a fire, an accident, or an act of violence—with the idea of selling such photos to a local newspaper. The money that the photographer receives is hardly worth his effort. What he does want is a credit line, printed acknowledgment that he took the photo. This type of identification can be an effective means of helping a photographer acquire a reputation.

The exhibition is another way photographers use to achieve recognition. Many libraries, banks, and department stores are happy to display the works of photographers. Some small theaters have galleries that are ideal for such a purpose. The pictures the photographer selects for exhibit are usually built around a central theme, if possible one that relates to the community. "The City at Night" or "Back to School" are typical exhibition subjects.

Wagner International Photos, Inc., of New York City, an agency that specializes in photography of all types for major corporations, advertising agencies, and public relations firms, presents an annual public relations seminar. Panelists are well-known journalists. Invited guests are New York's public relations executives. By sponsoring this meeting ground for public relations professionals and media representatives, Wagner International builds its reputation and renown.

Photographs can be taken by anyone with a camera and film, and literally billions of them are taken each year. But many agencies are encountering real difficulty in recruiting and hiring capable photographers.

"We're always on the lookout for qualified people," says Gary Wagner, president of Wagner International. "But being qualified means much more than simply knowing how to use a camera.

"When I interview a photographer for a job, the first thing I check is his appearance. Is he neat, clean, and well-dressed? I can't send a shaggy-haired photographer on an assignment to take a picture of the president of U.S. Steel.

"After appearance, personality is next in importance. The job candidate has to be able to impress me that he has the ability to deal with people of different types, and be able to maintain a pleasant disposition no matter what demands the assignment makes upon him.

"If the young man is qualified as far as appearance and temperament are concerned, I then check his skills. What experience has he had? What types of equipment is he capable of using? I look at his sample portfolio. I check his references."

Finding qualified photographers is only one of the personnel difficulties studio owners face. "Getting people to work at developing film and printing is also becoming a problem," says Gary Wagner.

"Nowadays when a young man begins thinking of a career in photography, he invariably thinks in terms of the glamor side of the business, of becoming a photographer. No one wants to start by being a darkroom assistant anymore."

The setting of fees is an extremely important matter in the operation of a studio or agency. No studio can be successful unless the owner receives an adequate return for the work performed. How much do professional photographers charge? Photographer Joseph Breitenbach, of New York City, who numbers American Telephone & Telegraph Co., Eastman Kodak Company, and IBM among his clients, receives as much as $1,000 for a single color photograph. At the other end of the scale is the young photographer who is seeking to become established. He might take a series of

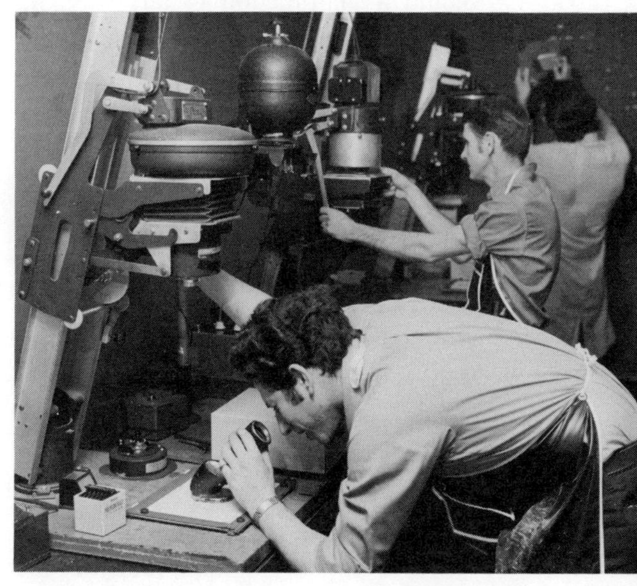

Equipping the darkroom and staffing it are part of the studio owner's responsibility

103

photographs for a publication, and if in payment he receives only a credit line, he is content. Fees cover an extremely wide range!

To determine a schedule of fees, the studio owner begins by estimating his annual fixed costs—his rent, payroll, insurance, and office expenses. He also has to figure how much his equipment will depreciate in a year.

The equipment needed to run a photo studio is no minor item. Every photographer employed by the studio requires two or three different cameras, and at least two "bodies" of each type. No photographer leaves the studio for an assignment without at least one spare body of the type of camera he is to use. Should he drop or jar his camera and damage it, or should it malfunction in any way, he simply switches lenses to the spare body.

Even a photographer working in a studio needs at least one reserve camera of the type he is using. A client or an assistant could trip over his tripod, throwing the camera to the floor. He can't put off the assignment until the camera is repaired; he has to have a backup.

For portrait photography, most studios use a camera that produces a negative that is 4″ × 5″ or larger in size.

On most assignments outside the studio, the photographer uses a 35mm. camera. It is easy to operate and inexpensive in terms of film costs. When it comes to 35mm. camera, many com-

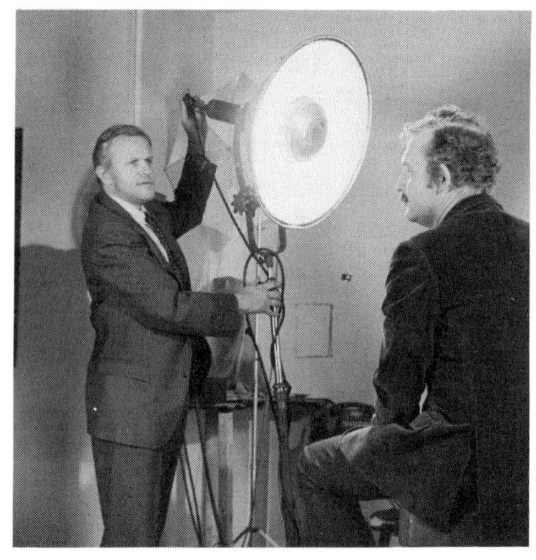

Besides cameras, lights are part of the equipment every studio requires

mercial photographers prefer the Nikon, which costs about $250.

The cost of cameras is really only the beginning. Photographers need special lenses. They need light meters and these, like cameras, have to be purchased in duplicate.

Flood lamps, equipped with special dimmers, and light stands are needed, as well as electronic flash equipment.

Film costs also have to be reflected in a studio's fees. Studios nowadays use more 35mm. film than any other type. Film of this size is packed in individual steel cylinder-shaped cartridges called cassettes. Each cassette holds film enough to take thirty-six photos. Most manufacturers of film design their cassettes so they cannot be reused. The only reasonable alternative is to purchase cassettes in large quantities, for manufacturers give dis-

104

counts on bulk purchases. Most studios will purchase two to four months' supply of film at a time.

The film has to be stored where it is cool and dry, otherwise it deteriorates. Many studios use a refrigerator for film storage. It is the ideal place.

Nearly every commercial studio develops its own black-and-white film and prints its own pictures, so the studio owner must keep an accurate accounting of how much he spends for chemicals and printing paper, and these expenses must also be reflected in the studio's fees. Many commercial studios buy chemicals in powdered form and mix small quantities as they are needed. Powdered chemicals are less expensive than liquid, and they are easier to store and keep longer.

The processing of color film requires expensive equipment and specially trained technicians. Almost all studios employ the services of a custom laboratory to do their color work.

Insurance is another expense the photo studio must bear. Suppose a light explodes while the photographer is taking a portrait, and the flying glass injures the subject. Or the photographer drops a piece of equipment from a tall building and it strikes a pedestrian. The damage claims that might result could plunge the studio owner into bankruptcy. To protect himself against such occurrences, he buys liability insurance.

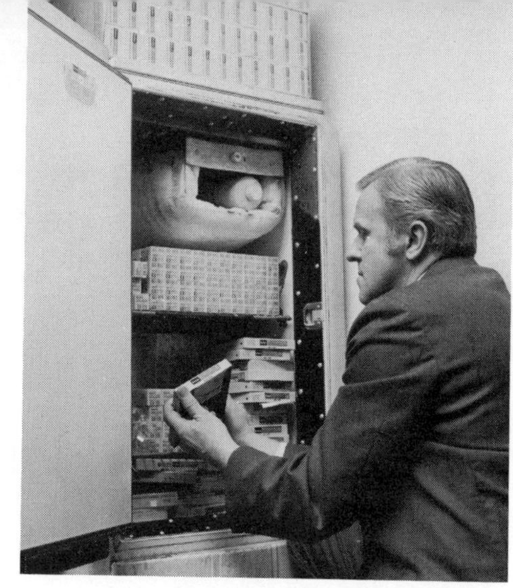

Film has to be stored where it is cool and dry

He must also purchase insurance to guard against fire and theft. The amount he buys has to be enough to replace equipment that might be damaged, destroyed, or stolen.

The fee charged for a photo assignment must reimburse the studio for the photographer's time, and for any expenses he might incur in getting to and from the assignment. The fee must also reflect any out of the ordinary expenses that might be involved. Perhaps it was a Sunday job and required the payment of overtime. Last, the fee must include a sum that represents a fair profit for the studio.

But the rewards of operating a photo studio are more than financial. There's the sense of pride that comes in having taken a distinctive photograph, a satisfaction offered by few other business enterprises.

10

POLICE PRECINCT HOUSE

To prevent and detect crime, and to enforce the laws—these are the police department's chief responsibilities. To carry out these responsibilities, the department relies upon its precinct houses. No large city could be adequately protected without them.

A precinct is simply a geographical area of a city. The precinct house, often called a station house, is the headquarters for police activity in an area. A city may have only a handful of precincts or scores of them. It depends upon the city's size and the amount of territory to be covered.

Each station house is commanded by a high-ranking officer, usually a captain or a lieutenant. His chief responsibility is directing the patrolmen assigned to the precinct.

Patrol itself is the most important function of any police department. Experts in crime prevention say that two conditions must exist before a crime takes place. First, a person must have a desire to commit a misdeed; second, he must believe the opportunity exists to get away with it. The police officer on patrol removes the second condition. Any area that is frequently and conspicuously patrolled is likely to have a low crime rate.

The city of London was the first to establish a police patrol. Sir Robert Peel's Metropolitan Police Act of 1829 created a uniform force of patrol officers to cover the entire city, day and night. Within the next few decades, almost every major city in the world followed London's lead.

At any given station house, more officers are involved in patrol than in any other duty. Some patrol on foot, others in vehicles.

Each precinct is divided into areas called "beats." Normally, the same foot patrolmen cover the same beat each day. Patrol cars cover larger areas of the precinct called "sectors."

The advantage of foot patrol is that it puts the police officer in close contact with the people. But the foot patrolman lacks mobility and he can cover only a limited part of a precinct. The patrol car, on the other hand, can respond rapidly to emergency calls. It can carry several police officers, a radio, riot guns, first-aid equipment, and fire extinguishers. It is practically a mobile police station.

In New York City, each station house also has its own motor scooter squad. Scooter patrol was introduced in 1966, and is now considered indispensable for patrolling parks, piers, beaches, and other little-traveled areas of a precinct that cannot be easily covered by foot patrolmen or radio cars.

Scooter patrol combines the advantage of foot patrol, putting the police officer in close contact with the people, with the quick response and mobility of the radio car. New York's scooter patrolmen—there are more than 3,000 of them—have been re-sponsible for countless arrests, rescues, and lifesaving acts.

Scooter patrolmen wear special equipment, including protective helmets and, during periods of darkness, luminous belts. Scooters are not operated when the weather is bad or when high winds prevail.

The two-wheeled motorcycle is considered too heavy for use in heavy traffic, and few precinct houses have them. Besides, they are costly to operate. Less dangerous is the three-wheeled motorcycle, sometimes used in enforcing parking regulations by officers checking parking meter time limits and tagging illegally parked automobiles, or any other task where frequent dismounting is necessary.

The patrolmen assigned to a precinct usually work shifts of eight hours' duration. Well before his tour of duty begins, each patrolman arrives at the station house to jot down alarms in his memo book. Alarms are messages received by teletype from central communications which give facts about wanted persons, missing persons, and stolen automobiles.

Just before leaving the station house, the men going on duty assemble in the muster room. Any urgent matters are brought to their attention, and they stand inspection. The precinct commanding officer checks uniforms to see that they are neat, clean, and unwrinkled. Firearms, flashlights, handcuffs, and any leather-covered equipment must show diligent care.

One expert in police work says that

Before their tour of duty begins, patrolmen note alarms in their memo books

A sergeant briefs the men going on patrol

A sergeant makes an entry in the precinct house arrest book

the work of a patrolman is mainly observation. His power to observe enables him to discover wanted persons and stolen cars. By keen observation he can appraise situations and conditions that produce crime.

The man on patrol is to the police what the combat soldier is to the army, the man on the firing line. Often he is the first to arrive at the scene of a crime or emergency. He must know how to act when confronted by an accident, a suicide attempt, drowning, or childbirth.

Besides his enormous value in helping to prevent crime, the policeman on patrol performs many other services. He may be asked to call an ambulance for a sick person, keep angry people from fighting, or help a lost child. He is constantly aiding people in distress. When his tour of duty is over, the patrolman returns to the precinct house to set down his observa-

tions and investigations in written reports to his superiors.

Each precinct is also staffed by detectives. The detective squad is much smaller than the patrol force. Some detectives specialize in the apprehension of burglars. Others may be assigned to the department's homicide squad; they investigate murders. Most large cities have detective service twenty-four hours a day.

The nerve center for all precinct operations is the desk, actually a long, high counter. Located just beyond the main entrance to the station house, the desk is manned by a high-ranking officer and a staff of two or three men. All the precinct's communications facilities are close at hand.

When somebody is arrested by one of the precinct patrolmen or a detective, he is brought before the desk to be "booked," that is, the prisoner's name and address and the nature of the

108

crime he committed are entered in the station house's arrest book. Crimes are classified as either misdemeanors or felonies. A misdemeanor is the less serious of the two. Reckless driving is one example of a misdemeanor. A felony is a serious crime, such as robbery, burglary, or murder. A prisoner who has committed a felony is fingerprinted and is likely to be questioned by a police detective at the time he is booked.

Many precinct houses have detention cells. They are used to hold prisoners overnight, or until they can be brought to court for a hearing.

As soon as it is reasonably possible, the prisoner is brought before a magistrate who has the power to try minor offenses and hold preliminary examinations in the case of felonies. If the judge decides there is reason to believe the arrested person committed the felony, he is jailed and a date is set for his trial. He can be released from custody by posting bail, a sum of money established by the judge which the prisoner gives over to the court as a guarantee that he will return at the appointed time.

Most police departments in large cities have started community relations programs in recent years. Each precinct is likely to have its own community relations council, the members representing a cross section of the precinct's community life. School officials, business leaders, clergymen, leaders of block associations, and neighborhood organizations may all be involved.

Council meetings provide an opportunity for people in a community to get to know one another and to get to know their police. Council committees perform a variety of services. They have conducted street festivals and antipoverty projects. They have provided countless opportunities for groups of city youngsters to spend a summer day at a beach or amusement park. Many councils stress sports programs for young people.

In New York City, each precinct has its own community relations patrolmen to stimulate council activity. The precinct commanding officer attends all council meetings.

"I think the most important function a community council has is to simply help maintain harmony in the neighborhood," says one police official. "And often the council works remarkably

A patrolman checks the complaint board before going on duty

Call boxes are often used to report crimes

room. Information about the crime is fed into a computer by the man receiving the call. Instantly the computer pinpoints the precinct involved, the patrol sector within the precinct, and reports the nearest available patrol cars.

Within two or three seconds, this information is flashed onto a screen in front of the radio dispatcher, the police officer who is in charge of assigning patrol cars. He sends one or more cars to the crime scene. Patrol cars are equipped with two-way radio, so they can report on action taken. Each one of the precinct's foot patrolmen is linked to the dispatcher by means of a walkie-talkie unit he carries.

SPRINT—for *S*pecial *P*olice *R*adio *I*nquiry *Net*work—is the name of this modern communications system. More

well in doing this. It helps expose false rumors and put facts in proper perspective. It corrects wrong ideas that people have about the police, and about one another too."

Although the precinct house is the control center for police operations in a given area, it does not function as an independent unit. Far from it. Each one of the precinct's foot patrolmen and patrol cars is linked to a central communications point.

In New York City, the system works like this: A person who needs police help dials 911, the special police emergency number. An automatic call distributor feeds the call to one of a corps of 24 men in central communications

Calls are received at this station house switchboard

110

than 15,000 New Yorkers dial 911 each day.

New York City residents can also report crimes or emergency situations by means of call boxes posted at convenient locations in each precinct. These calls are received at a switchboard in each station house, as are telephone calls placed directly to the precinct. When the police officer at the switchboard receives a call, he consults a map to determine which patrol sector of the precinct is involved, and then radios the alarm to the appropriate patrol car.

Today's station house is much different from what it used to be. It still serves as headquarters for the precinct patrol officers and detectives, where records of crimes are maintained. But nowadays the station house is a sophisticated communications center as well.

This is the radio dispatcher. Stationed at the communications headquarters, he assigns patrol cars to the crime scene

11

DEPARTMENT STORE

WHEN A PERSON from a foreign country comes to the United States for the first time, the American department store never fails to be high up on the list of things that impress him the most. The dazzling variety of merchandise, prepackaged and displayed so attractively, and the uncounted services these stores offer are taken for granted by most Americans, but they are as unique to this country as professional football.

As its name says, a department store is a large retail store that is organized into sections called "departments," each one stocking and selling a different type of merchandise. Many people look upon each one of the country's tens of thousands of general merchandise stores as "department stores," but the U.S. Department of the Census limits the use of the name to stores with 25 or more employees. There are approximately 4,000 stores of this type.

About half the country's department stores are located in large cities, and the other half in suburban shopping centers. Indeed, the dominant store in

New York's Macy's is the largest department store in the world. It covers a full city block

every large shopping center is usually a department store.

The department store is similar to the supermarket in its size and in the multitude of products it offers, yet the department store is organized in a much different manner. The supermarket is organized along product lines. A manager is in charge of the store, and supervisors representing groceries, meat, and produce report to him. But the department store is organized according to functions, not products. A general manager is in charge of the store. He has supervisors in charge of each one of the following functions: control, personnel, sales promotion, operations, and merchandising.

The control department is concerned with the store's finances. It employs bookkeepers and accountants to maintain the store's financial records. It also issues payments to the store's suppliers and prepares the employee payroll. The personnel department recruits and hires store employees.

The sales promotion department plans and executes the store's advertising programs. It is also concerned with special events, like fashion shows and instruction classes. The operations department is responsible for the store building, for the physical plant. It takes care of heating and air conditioning, and maintenance and repair.

The merchandising unit is in charge of all selling and buying. It is the most important department of all in terms of store income.

One distinctive feature of the department store is that its various *merchandise* departments—women's coats and suits, menswear, home furnishings, sporting goods, toys, and all the others—are operated independently of one another. Each is headed by a manager, and each has its own buyer or buyers, who are responsible for purchasing merchandise for the department. Each

Department stores are noted for the wide variety of merchandise they offer

merchandise department also maintains its own records of sales and expenses. It is almost as if the merchandise department were a small store in itself.

Some departments of the store are not operated by store personnel, but are leased to individuals or companies. This is particularly true in the case of jewelry and drugs and other merchandise, the selling of which requires specialized knowledge and experience. The leased department is usually operated under the name of the store, and conforms to store policies in selling and advertising. To the everyday customer, the leased department looks no different from any other.

Meticulous planning goes into the layout of a department store. Store officials look upon the various aisles in the same way a traffic engineer views highways and streets. Some aisles, because of their location and width, are main traffic arteries. Other aisles have only secondary importance.

Some store departments may be leased to individuals or companies

Any aisle that receives heavy traffic is likely to display "impulse" merchandise, items that a customer is likely to purchase on the spur of the moment, without prior planning or special need. Cosmetics, costume jewelry, gloves, and hosiery are often classified as impulse items. They are usually to be found along the main aisle leading from the store's main entrance.

Impulse buying is usually done under hurried conditions, but some other types of merchandise are purchased only after considerable planning on the part of the customer and are almost never sold in a hurried fashion. China, silverware, and expensive jewelry are examples of merchandise of this type. Departments selling these goods are likely to be found away from the mainstream of traffic, where leisurely buying is possible.

According to another rule of depart-ment store layout, merchandise that brings a customer into a store must be made relatively inaccessible. Suppose a department store advertises women's coats at reduced prices. Women attracted to the store by the advertisement would not be likely to find the coats on the first floor near the main entrance. The chances are that the coats would be at the far end of the store, or on an upper floor. To get to the coats, the women would have to pass through many departments displaying impulse merchandise.

The "shoppe" arrangement is a layout plan that has been gaining in popularity in recent years. Under this concept, a department is created from various types of merchandise that are related in use. A typical shoppe might be called "Leisure World." Here store customers would find adult games and puzzles, film and camera equipment, painting and art supplies, and health and sports equipment.

In newer department stores, the center area of each floor is the selling zone. Partitions are erected around its outside edge to enclose a space ten to twenty feet in depth. This space is used to store merchandise. If a sales-clerk does not have an item a customer wants, she can quickly get it from the storage area. This layout plan suggests why modern department stores do not have windows.

Customers often choose to shop in department stores because of the many different services they offer. One of these is a complaint and adjustment service. When a customer makes a purchase and later finds it to be unsatisfactory, she counts on being able to exchange the item, or to have her account credited in the amount of the purchase, or to receive a cash refund. Some stores allow department managers to handle complaints and adjustments. Other stores establish a central complaint department for all merchandise.

Delivery is another service the department store is expected to provide. Large department stores own and operate their own fleets of delivery trucks. Smaller stores within the same trading area often mutually own and operate a single fleet of trucks, each store sharing costs in proportion to its use.

All department stores offer credit too. A customer who makes a purchase expects to be allowed an extended period of time to make payment, if she wishes.

Many stores offer expert advice by decorators, at no charge to customers. A bridal consultant helps the prospective bride arrange everything from the style of type for the wedding invitation to the length of her gown. There are free fashion shows, advice on the use of cosmetics and hair styling, and classes in sewing and knitting.

Store managers rate personal selling as a service too. When you shop in a supermarket, you are not assisted; it is *self*-service. But when you shop in a department store, you become involved in what is known as the "selling process," a carefully developed series of actions that begin when you approach a counter and end when you have made your purchase and leave the store.

Experts in retail selling recognize that there are two different types of customers. The first type knows exactly what he wants when he enters the store. With this type, the salesperson's job is merely to satisfy the customer's desire by providing the right merchandise.

The second type of customer has only a general idea of what he wants. He may be "just looking." In this case, the salesperson must do more of a selling job, showing the customer the items available and describing the advantages of each. The salesperson is trained to distinguish between the two types, and he adjusts his selling technique accordingly.

Suppose you enter a department store to buy a pair of shoes. The selling process would involve these steps:

The "shoppe" arrangement is a layout concept many modern stores follow

You should first be greeted by the salesclerk as you entered the shoe department. Then the clerk would try to find out your needs, getting as much detailed information as possible—your shoe size and the style and color you prefer.

The second step in the selling process is to present the merchandise. The clerk will show you a pair of shoes and invite you to examine them. "Get the goods into the customer's hands" is a fundamental piece of advice department managers give their clerks.

Next the clerk will encourage you to try on the shoes. While assisting you, he is likely to mention that the shoes are well made and durable, and that they are stylish. "They're the latest thing," he is likely to say.

The fourth stage occurs when you begin to resist the sale; everyone does to some degree. A well-trained salesperson recognizes two types of objections. The first type takes the form of an excuse and often has no direct bearing on the merchandise being purchased. For example, you are using excuse-type objection when you tell the clerk, "I'll think it over and come back tomorrow," or, "I have to talk it over with my parents." The clerk realizes that you have some objection to the shoes, but you don't wish to state it. You may feel that they do not look well on you or that the price is too high. At any rate, you wish to put off any decision to buy. Sales resistance of this type is hard to overcome.

But if you have what is termed a "real objection" to the merchandise, a good salesman will not be distressed. He will be able to turn your objection into a selling point. Suppose you say, "These shoes cost too much. I can buy them cheaper elsewhere."

The salesman is likely to answer, "Of course, you can buy cheaper shoes, but you wouldn't get the value you're getting with these shoes." And with that he would launch into a description of the shoes' leading features. In other words, your objection—price—is turned into a reason for buying.

Once the salesperson has overcome your resistance, the last step is to close the sale. In this phase, the salesperson is likely to help you in narrowing down your choice to just two pairs of shoes, and then he helps you to make the final selection. In doing this, he is likely to point out that a particular pair of shoes is comfortable, looks well on you, is made of quality materials, and will be long-wearing. Step by step he leads you into a decision to buy.

If you hesitate about making up your mind, the salesperson has several ways of coaxing you. He may ask you a direct question, such as, "Do you wish to take these with you, or shall I have them sent?" Or he may say, "Do you wish to pay cash, or is this a charge?" Questions like these quickly bring the sale to a close.

Other times the salesperson will trigger a favorable buying decision by presenting a choice. For example, he may ask you, "Do you want the brown pair or the black ones?" Or he may say,

"Do you want the low-priced pair, or do you prefer the more expensive ones?"

Occasionally a salesperson will try to prompt a customer to buy by stressing that an item is in short supply. He may say, "This style is going fast. We have just a few pairs left in your size and we don't expect any more." Claims of this type appeal to many people. Of course, no reputable store uses such a method of persuasion unless the statement is absolutely true.

The salesperson may also seek to close the sale by stressing that the merchandise can be charged or sent C.O.D. (cash on delivery). He may also refer to the store's refund policy. "We stand behind these shoes," he may say. "If you find you're not happy with them, bring them back. We'll refund your money."

Once you make your decision to buy, the salesperson records the sale and wraps your purchase. During this stage, he may suggest additional items to go along with your purchase. If you have just bought a pair of shoes, the salesperson may suggest a can of polish or shoe trees. Or he may tell you, "This week we're having a special sale on hosiery."

But whether you decide to purchase additional merchandise or not, the salesperson usually completes the sale by complimenting you on your choice and thanking you. "Won't you come in again?" may be his parting words.

The department store wants you to leave the store with a feeling of satisfaction. If you do not feel fully satisfied, the store feels that the salesperson has not been successful. That is why a reputable store will give only truthful information about its merchandise. Its sales personnel will be courteous and efficient in dealing with you; they will show appreciation for the sale, and make any necessary adjustments. One department store manager gives his sales personnel this advice: "Always treat the customer as an honored guest."

Like any service, personal selling costs, and more than a few experts in retail selling are beginning to question this cost in terms of value received. One day department stores may be largely self-service stores.

Store managers now realize that the self-service system gives the shopper a chance to look around at her leisure, unbothered by a salesperson. The shopper sees, evaluates, and purchases merchandise she might not choose otherwise. "Self-service often accomplishes as much as the experienced salesperson and more than the mediocre salesclerk," says one expert in the field. Many leading department stores have already converted portions of their selling zones to self-service operation, and hundreds of other stores are expected to make such conversions in the future.

Selling merchandise is the key to a department store's profit, but few sales would be made without sales promotion, an operation that includes advertising, publicity, public relations, special events, in-store displays—anything that makes people want to buy.

Of all the methods that department stores use to promote sales, newspaper advertising is the one they prefer. According to the National Retail Dry Goods Association, 54 percent of the average store's promotion budget goes toward newspaper advertising. Next highest on the list is in-store displays, commanding 15 percent of the budget. Radio and television advertising and direct mail promotion each get about 3 percent.

Department stores prefer newspapers as an advertising medium because the readership of a local daily newspaper is likely to include people of both sexes, all ages, and a wide range of incomes and educational levels. No matter what kind of merchandise the store advertises, it is sure to reach prospective customers through the newspaper.

Another advantage is that the readers of a newspaper live in a compact, well-defined geographical area. This intense coverage contrasts with that of radio or television programs. Since different programs appeal to different types of people, the audience is often "fragmented."

The newspaper advertising message can be of almost any size, from a small portion of one page to many pages. With radio and television, commercials are limited in length.

Of course, department stores do use radio and television in their sales promotion efforts. Many stores have found television especially valuable. The medium allows the store to do personal selling, with an announcer explaining, demonstrating, and selling a product, all at the same time. But television time is expensive to buy, and often it is used only to supplement a newspaper campaign.

Direct mail is advertising sent through the post office. One reason department stores use this type of advertising is that it is selective. The sales promotion department can decide in advance who is to receive the advertising. Perhaps they wish to confine the mailing only to those people who live within three miles of the store, or limit it to the store's charge account customers.

Direct mail is also flexible as to the size and form of the advertising. The mailing piece can be as simple as a postcard, or multicolored with many pages.

And direct mail advertising does not depend upon a newspaper's publication date or the broadcast schedule of a radio or television station. It is sent out exactly when the store wishes. "With direct mail, the store is always in control," is the way one advertising manager puts it.

Displays are one of the most powerful forms of sales promotion. Some stores estimate that 30 to 40 percent of their sales come about as a direct result of displays.

There are two types of store displays. One is window display. In large department stores, window display is considered so important that a display manager is employed to work with buyers and department managers in

All stores rely on interior display to sell merchandise

creating and decorating store windows.

The other type of display is interior display. This refers to merchandise shown on counters or tables, or in racks or showcases. In a large department store, one salesperson in each department is responsible for his department's interior display.

Window displays are not only important in selling merchandise, but they also have value in establishing a store's character. The windows of a store noted for its smartness are likely to display the latest in women's fashions. A store that is highly esteemed in a community will display merchandise in a simple and sedate manner. A store that appeals to many types of customers may crowd its windows with a great assortment of merchandise.

The window displays of many department stores have a genuine artistic quality, and the principles of line and design are emphasized in each window, just as if the display manager were creating a fine painting or a piece of sculpture. There is always harmony of sizes and color, and the objects are arranged in pleasing relationships.

Color is used to create moods and express ideas, with the emphasis almost always on somber shades or gray tones. These are used with dashes of more intense colors. Usually one color dominates.

Notice that when you look at a window display your eye is drawn immediately to a focal point, a center of interest, and then to the less important details. Window display experts have many ways of accentuating one idea or object. They may achieve this by arrangement, by a special way of grouping the objects that are presented. Or they may use color as a means of emphasis, displaying a light object against a dark background, for instance. Or the display may accent one object over many by the clever use of space, by using a sizable amount of open area around the object.

Ideas for window displays are gleaned from many sources. Fads, current events, plays, books, or motion pictures may provide the basic subject matter. Often window displays are related to upcoming seasons or holidays. New York City's department stores are renowned for their Christmas windows, and people travel many hundreds of miles to see them. Just one window may represent the expenditure of several thousands of dollars.

Most department stores follow the policy of creating simple displays and changing them frequently, at least once a week. Few stores ever repeat a display, no matter how successful it has proved to be.

You will never see the window of a fashionable store being changed—"dressed." It is not considered in good taste. Window-dressing is done at night, after the store has closed, or the job is done behind austere window shades. The windows of one New York City department store can be lowered to the basement where they are dressed.

In recent years, more and more attention has been directed toward interior displays. Departments that sell furniture, toys, chinaware, glassware, household wares, appliances, and rugs have become vast exhibition areas. If a department store's windows feature a specific type of merchandise—leather goods, for instance—the window display is likely to be reproduced in the leather goods department as a reminder to the customer.

Interior displays are not changed as often as window displays. But store managers realize that varying a department's displays is a proven method of boosting sales.

Customers are constantly picking up and examining displayed merchandise, so store personnel have to keep a watchful eye on interior displays to be sure they do not become disordered. An untidy display has a harmful effect upon sales. However, a well-trained salesclerk will never improve a display in the presence of a customer. It might make him feel unwelcome.

A department store often uses many different types of sales promotion simultaneously to make people want to buy. On the same day newspaper advertising appears for a particular item, store windows feature it, and the item is also prominently displayed in the appropriate department. In addition, letters or brochures announcing the offering are sent to the store's customers.

Selling is one of the two principal aspects of department store operation. Buying is the other. It is equal in importance and just as much of an art.

In retail buying, three factors are important: how much to buy, what kind to buy, and when to buy. Department store buyers follow certain guidelines in making their buying decisions. They first establish whether the item being purchased represents staple merchandise or fashion merchandise.

Furniture displays may include complete model rooms like this one

120

Staples are those goods which fulfill a basic need. Often they are classed as necessities. Food is the most noted of staples. Towels, mattresses, blankets, and men's undershirts—these are examples of department store staples.

Fashion merchandise is quite different. It is characterized by a distinctiveness in style that customers feel is important. Nearly every item of women's wearing apparel is considered fashion merchandise.

Both staple and fashion merchandise are also classified as to demand. For some items, the demand is strictly seasonal. For others, it is uniform throughout the year.

The easiest type of merchandise to buy is staple merchandise that is constantly in demand, or without seasonal influence. The buyer merely has to keep a close check on the amount of the item he has in stock. When the inventory of the item falls below a certain level, he orders. The size of the order is based upon the expected demand, which the buyer estimates from store sales records of previous years.

Buying merchandise that is staple in character but seasonal in demand is not difficult either. In this case, the buyer has only to anticipate the period of peak demand. Take boys' undershirts as an example. The buyer knows that during the last two weeks of August and the first week of September sales of boys' undershirts will reach a peak because mothers are outfitting their youngsters for the school year. From the store's records, he knows exactly

New York City department stores are noted for their spectacular window displays at Christmastime

how many undershirts were sold in the August–September period the year before. He is likely to order a quantity slightly over that amount.

Of course, the demand for undershirts may not reach the level he has anticipated. Then cartons of undershirts will fill the warehouse. But with a staple item, even one that is sold on somewhat of a seasonal basis, this is not a serious problem. Since the demand for staple merchandise is continuous, the undershirts will eventually be sold.

But in buying fashion merchandise, the buyer must exercise a great deal more caution. He still must answer the three basic questions—how much, what kind, and when—but the wrong answer to any one can spell disaster. Ordering a fashion item in too great a quantity or ordering as the fashion is

121

diminishing in popularity can result in a warehouse being crammed with merchandise that may never be sold.

A fashion buyer must be able to forecast two trends, not just one. He must be able to predict when a fashion is about to become popular; then later he must be able to forecast when it is about to fall into disfavor. To be able to do this, a buyer requires astute knowledge of the history of fashion, and he must be shrewd and experienced in the art of negotiation. "A crystal ball also helps," says a buyer at one New York City store.

Some buyers follow what is called the "trickle down" theory in attempting to predict a fashion trend. It works like this: a new fashion will be created by a renowned Paris designer. It is then copied by designers of expensive "limited editions." Next, the fashion trickles down to the designers of lower-priced apparel, and ultimately it reaches the "mass appeal" markets. It is up to the buyer to perceive the trend at the very beginning of the cycle.

Sometimes a fashion cycle begins with a personality. For many years, Jacqueline Kennedy Onassis was regarded as a "fashion innovator," an "early adopter." When she was photographed wearing a pillbox hat in the spring of 1967, pillbox hats became an overnight fashion sensation.

During the late 1960's, the trickle-down theory began to be questioned. "Paris and personalities may still be the guiding light for some women," says a buyer at a New York department store, "but most people today dress according to their likes and dislikes. Today's women happen to like the miniskirt, and they aren't going to have their minds changed about it by any Paris designer or Jackie Onassis."

It would seem that the department store buyer of today is faced with an almost impossible task. From all the various styles and fashions being offered, how can he possibly select the ones that are going to be popular?

His most important source of information comes from his suppliers. A department store buyer may be in contact with as many as twenty different salesmen when doing his ordering, and they provide a constant flow of intelligence about fashions and styles.

Sometimes a group of stores will establish what is known as a "resident buying office." The office is staffed by specialists in such lines as apparel or home furnishings to advise the store buyers as to consumer preferences.

Trade magazines and merchandise exhibitions also help. Finally, a smart buyer maintains continuing contact with the customers of his department to learn their likes and dislikes.

BIBLIOGRAPHY

Chapter 1 BOWLING CENTER

Bowling Center Maintenance Standards. Washington, D.C.: The National Bowling Council, 1967.

Reich, Carl, "Adults Take a Back Seat," *Bowling Magazine,* Seventeenth Yearbook Issue, September, 1969.

Chapter 2 COMMUNITY PHARMACY

Gladwell, Lloyd, *Starting and Managing a Small Retail Drugstore.* Washington, D.C.: Small Business Administration, 1966.

Mathison, Richard, *The Eternal Search: The Story of Man and His Drugs.* New York: G. P. Putnam's Sons, 1958.

Chapter 3 SKI AREA

Auran, John Henry, "Schools Are Big Business at Mt. Tom," *Skiing Area News,* Fall, 1969.

Buyce, Gerry, "At Belleayre, Our Snow Is Cultivated," *Skiing Area News,* January, 1968.

Jackson, Myles, "Summer Business, Key to Year-round Success," *Ski Area Management,* Winter, 1969.

Chapter 4 RESTAURANT

Fairbook, Paul, *Starting and Managing a Small Restaurant.* Washington, D.C.: Small Business Administration, 1964.

Westbrook, James H., *Aim for a Job in Restaurants and Food Service.* New York: Richards Rosen Press, Inc., 1969.

Chapter 5 SUMMER CAMP

Joy, Barbara Ellen, *Camping.* Minneapolis: Burgess Publishing Company, 1957.

Proud, Dorothy M., "Food Costs and Menu Planning," *Camping Magazine,* February, 1966.

Reimann, Lewis C., *The Successful Camp.* Ann Arbor: The University of Michigan Press, 1958.

Chapter 6   CHAIN SUPERMARKET

Brand, Edward A., *Modern Supermarket Operation.* New York: Fairchild Publications, Inc., 1963.
Charvat, Frank J., *Supermarketing.* New York: The Macmillan Company, 1961.
Mund, Vernon A., *Open Markets: An Essential of Free Enterprise.* New York: Harper & Brothers, 1948.
Personnel Training Handbook: Managers in Training. Brooklyn, N.Y.: New York State Food Merchants Association, 1963.
"The Supermarket of the 1970's," *Progressive Grocer,* June, 1969.

Chapter 7   GENERAL AVIATION AIRPORT

Bibbern, Donald S., *Starting and Managing an Aviation Fixed Base Operation.* Washington, D.C.: Small Business Administration (no date).
The Airport—Its Influence on the Community Economy. Washington, D.C.: Systems Planning Division, Federal Aviation Administration, 1967.
Utility Airports, Air Access to National Transportation. Washington, D.C.: Federal Aviation Administration, November, 1968.

Chapter 8   TELEVISION STATION

Lawton, Sherman P., *The Modern Broadcaster.* New York: Harper & Brothers, 1961.
Quall, Ward L., and Martin, Leo A., *Broadcast Management: Radio-Television.* New York: Hastings House, Publishers, Inc., 1966.
Roe, Yale (ed.), *Television Station Management.* New York: Hastings House, Publishers, Inc., 1964.
Television Fact Book. Washington, D.C.: Television Digest, Inc., 1968–1969.
Winick, Charles, "The Television Station Manager," *Advanced Management Journal,* January, 1966.

Chapter 9   COMMERCIAL PHOTOGRAPHY SERVICE

Gutenberg, Arthur W., and Albrecht, Val, *Profitable Studio Management.* New York: American Photographic Book Publishing Co., Inc., 1965.
Schwarz, Theodore, *The Business Side of Photography.* New York: American Photographic Book Publishing Co., Inc., 1969.

Chapter 10   POLICE PRECINCT HOUSE

"New Station House Opens," *Spring 3100,* September, 1955.
Wilson, O. W., *Police Administration.* New York: McGraw-Hill Book Company, Inc., 1963.

Chapter 11   DEPARTMENT STORE

Gist, Ronald R., *Retailing: Concepts and Decisions.* New York: John Wiley & Sons, Inc., 1968.
Hess, Max, Jr., *Every Dollar Counts: The Story of the American Department Store.* New York: Fairchild Publications, Inc., 1952.
Retailing. Washington, D.C.: Small Business Administration, 1969.
Robinson, O. Preston, *Store Salesmanship.* Englewood Cliffs, N.J.: Prentice-Hall, Inc., 1966.

INDEX